★ ★ ★ ★ ★ ★ ★ ★ ★ ★ ★ ★ ★ ★

This book is from
the kitchen library
of

_____Penny_____

★ ★ ★ ★ ★ ★ ★ ★ ★ ★ ★ ★ ★ ★

ALSO BY ART GINSBURG, MR. FOOD®

The Mr. Food® Cookbook, OOH it's so GOOD!!™ (1990)

Mr. Food® Cooks Like Mama (1992)

Mr. Food® Cooks Chicken (1993)

Mr. Food® Cooks Pasta (1993)

Mr. Food® Makes Dessert (1993)

Mr. Food®'s Favorite Cookies (1994)

Mr. Food® Grills It All in a Snap (1995)

Mr. Food®'s Quick and Easy Side Dishes (1995)

Mr. Food®'s Fun Kitchen Tips and Shortcuts (and Recipes, Too!) (1995)

MR. FOOD®
Cooks

Real American

Art Ginsburg
MR. FOOD®

WILLIAM MORROW AND COMPANY, INC.

New York

Ginsburg, Art.
    Mr. Food cooks real American / Art Ginsburg. — 1st ed.
                    p.   cm.
              Includes index.
            ISBN 0-688-12637-5
        1. Cookery, American.   I. Title.
    TX715.G512   1994   94-20870
        641.5973—dc20   CIP

Printed in the United States of America

                7 8 9 10

BOOK DESIGN BY CHARLOTTE STAUB

Dedicated to
Margaret Spencer
and
Bertha Grotzky

Two teachers who supported me in
my early years and nurtured
my love of life and
performing.
Though they aren't here to witness
my success, I hope they are
looking down on me
with pride.

Acknowledgments

With a project as big as writing a cookbook, there are always so many people to thank. The ones who have really made this happen are Caryl Ginsburg Gershman, Steve Ginsburg, Roy Fantel, Carol Ginsburg, and Barbara Stevens.

I'd also like to thank my recipe testers, Linda Rose, Maria Zemantauski, Lori Puglisi, Terri Berkey, Madeline Burgan, and Loriann Bishop.

The contributions of Howard Rosenthal and Alice Palombo, the assistance of Mary Ann Oliver and Marilyn Ruderman, and, as always, the support of my wife, Ethel, son, Chuck, and the rest of our family, is greatly appreciated.

And once again, thanks to the gang at Morrow: Al Marchioni, Harriet Bell, Maria Guarnaschelli, and Skip Dye, who've stayed in there plugging with me. Thanks also to my agent, Bill Adler, who can always be counted on, and to a whiz of a publicist, Phyllis Heller.

A big thanks to so many of my friends all around the country who've offered their family secrets, family shortcuts, and family favorites. Plus, all of the companies that send me their newest (and sometimes oldest!) recipes, many of which I shorten up to make them as quick and easy as possible for our busy lifestyles. Thanks, folks. Let's keep sharing the **OOH it's so GOOD!!**™

More thanks to:

American Spice Trade Association
Baltimore Spice Company
Beef Industry Council
Bisquick® Baking Mix
Borden, Inc.
Butterball
California Prune Board
California Garlic Association
Chocolate Riesen® Caramels
Clear Springs Trout Company
Michael Cocca
Delmarva Poultry Industry, Inc.
The Florida Tomato Exchange
Ginny Gibbs
Hellmann's/Best Foods Mayonnaise
Joe's Stone Crab Restaurant

Kansas Beef Council

Keebler®

Kellogg USA

Kraft General Foods, Inc.

Marian Kurz

Joni Leterman

Lewis & Neale, Inc.

Lindsay Olive Growers

McCormick®/Schilling®

Mrs. Wilkes's Boarding House

The National Beef Cooking Contest

The National Beef Cook-Off

National Dairy Board

The National Pasta Association

The National Pork Producers Council

The National Turkey Federation

The New York Cherry Growers Association

The North Carolina Department of Agriculture

Kevin Nunn

Pace Foods

Pillsbury

Rawson, Inc.,
  makers of fine cabinetry

Redhot® Cayenne Pepper Sauce,
  a registered trademark of Reckitt & Colman Inc.

Restaurant Hospitality Magazine

Alan Roer

Sargento Cheese Co., Inc.

Deloris Simpson of Almost Heaven Bed & Breakfast

The South Florida Chili Cook-Off

Sunkist®

USA Dry Pea and Lentil Council

U.S.A. Rice Council

Valley Grower Magazine

Western New York Apple Growers Association

Wisconsin Milk Marketing Board

Glen Young

Poppy Seed Bread recipe,
  courtesy of *Homemade Good News Magazine* and Savannah Foods & Industries, Inc., makers of Dixie Crystals
  Sugar

Acknowledgments

Contents

Introduction

America—the home of diversity.
Troy, New York—the home of Uncle Sam . . . and me!

Growing up in Troy, New York, was the best! You wouldn't think that I'd have gotten much exposure to a variety of foods there, would you?

Well, I did! As a matter of fact, in my neighborhood alone, I had a world of taste experiences. Why, I could have had kielbasa and pierogi, flanken and potato pancakes, knockwurst and sauerkraut, and veal parmigiana with spaghetti all in the same day just by making the rounds of my friends' houses!

In fact, the first time I ever had lahmajoun (which I consider to be Armenian-style pizza—it's ground lamb on a thin dough, and it's un-believably tasty!) was at my friend Ann Osganian's house. Her mom had made a big stack of them and those first few bites were all I needed to push me on in search of more exciting food adventures!

Troy certainly did nurture my food love and curiosity. Those mixed neighborhoods, with their industrial and agricultural blend, gave me my Northeastern ethnic background, and as I spread my wings and experienced the local tastes of other areas, my curiosity grew even more. I've been "American fooding" ever after!

Since those early days, as I've traveled around the United States, I've been lucky enough to taste a variety of foods native to just about every area I've visited. What great opportunities I've had to sample every-thing from fresh Rhode Island tuna to grilled Cuban sandwiches in Miami's Little Havana . . . from real Texas barbecue in Kilgore, Texas, to New York pastrami, fresh California artichokes, and thick, creamy Boston clam chowder. (And, trust me—anybody who wants all the au-thentic tastes of Southern cooking can have them in one meal if they have lunch at Mrs. Wilkes's Boarding House in Savannah, Georgia. It's truly an experience not to be missed!)

Plus, I can't forget about the Kansas sorghum syrup over a stack of fluffy pancakes, or any of the hundreds of German sausages in Mil-waukee (and all those local Wisconsin cheeses). And how lucky can you be when right in Chicago you have every taste from Italian and Greek to the best "home on the range" steaks in the country!

But I know how lucky we *all* are to have the best of everything available to us. The food industry has to credit Frieda Caplan of Frieda's, Inc., of California for the awareness and wide availability of much of the newer exotic produce in most of our supermarkets now. And not only can we all enjoy foods like fresh kiwifruit and starfruit from other places, but now these are also being grown right here in the United States, because of their great popularity.

Our sweet summer onions are now widely available, too, because they're shipped to almost everywhere in the United States. No matter where we are we can have our Georgia Vidalias, Texas 1015s, California Imperials, Hawaiian Mauis, and Washington Walla Wallas. And we can all get fresh Southwestern-grown jalapeño peppers, Midwestern beef, Texas rice, and Louisiana hot pepper sauce.

Although fresh salmon is local in the Northwest, we can all enjoy it. And since California and Florida grow fresh produce all year long, we can benefit from that because availability no longer depends on our particular growing seasons or our proximity to field, stream, or ocean. The advances in growing, packing, and transporting our products have made all the difference in what we put on our dinner tables every night.

Now that these regional products are at our fingertips, why shouldn't we enjoy New England-style chowders, Southern-style gumbo and corn bread, and Tex-Mex-inspired guacamole and fajitas? From grits to cod to romaine, all of it's American. Now we can all enjoy all of America without leaving home!

I could go on and on about the wonderful foods our country has to offer! As always, I hope that you'll use my recipes as a place to start, a springboard to get you going in different directions. You have seen or will see many of them on my nationally syndicated MR. FOOD® television show. I always encourage you to do your own things to make the recipes your own. If you want to use different seasonings—fine. If you want to make substitutions—great! If you want to adapt them to be lighter, or to use less sugar, less salt, or less fat—wonderful! You've got to please *you*.

These recipes come from all over America. And, as always, they can be made from items out of your cupboard or right off your supermarket shelves. There are no expensive lists of specialty items here . . . uh-uh!

Introduction

There are smart shortcuts, hints, and tips already incorporated into the recipes.

So, go ahead and have fun. This book is about US and for US—you and me and everyone in the great U.S. . . . and beyond! ENJOY! And say

OOH it's so GOOD!!™

Did you know...

that Uncle Sam was a real person? He was!

Just like me, he was from Troy, New York. And just like me, he was a butcher. And since I grew up in Troy, I've got a real patriotic connection to Uncle Sam. That's why I've included him on the back of this book!

During the War of 1812, Samuel Wilson, a wholesale butcher in the then-village of Troy, New York, was popularly called "Uncle Sam." When he acquired a contract to supply meat to the army, he would stamp the barrels "U.S.," meaning United States, but the Troy soldiers referred to it as Uncle Sam's because it came from Uncle Sam Wilson. Well, more soldiers started picking up on the term "Uncle Sam's meat" and, as it spread throughout the country, everything government-owned was referred to as "Uncle Sam's" and it just grew and grew. Periodicals in the country started caricaturing the likeness with the stars and stripes, the beard, and the high hat, and it's been Uncle Sam/United States ever since.

Charts and Information

All-American Regional Menus

Need a different idea for a party or family get-together? Why not have dinner (or breakfast, brunch, or lunch) with a regional theme? You could do it yourself, or have everyone pitch in and make a different course!

Either way, you won't have to spend all day in the kitchen to wow them. You can have fun *and* be a hero! These are just a few menu ideas . . . go from here!

Southwestern

HORS D'OEUVRE
Full-of-Beans Dip (page 40) with tortilla chips

MAIN COURSE
Turkey Burritos (page 111)
or
Thirty-Minute Beef Chili (page 139)

ACCOMPANIMENTS
Santa Fe Rice Salad (page 174)
Fresh Salsa (page 61)

BREAD
Cayenne Corn Bread (page 220)

DESSERT
Lime Margarita Bars (page 257)

Charts and Information

New England

SOUP
New England Clam Chowder (page 81)

MAIN COURSE
Cod Cakes (page 146)
or
"Mapple" Roasted Ham (page 127)

ACCOMPANIMENTS
Succotash (page 212)
Cranberry Relish (page 57)
Not-So-Skinny Mashed Potatoes (page 168)

BREAD
Golden Herb Bread (page 223)

DESSERT
Grapenut Pudding (page 250)
and/or
Classic Deep-Dish Apple Pie (page 244)

Southern

SOUP
Pasta Gumbo (page 83)

MAIN COURSE
Mardi Gras Shrimp (page 149)
or
Key West Grilled Chicken (page 100)
or
Country-Fried Steak (page 124)

ACCOMPANIMENTS
Home-Fried Fresh Yams (page 166)
Florida Glazed Carrots and Parsnips (page 204)

BREAD
Peanut Muffins (page 227)

DESSERT
New Orleans Bread Pudding with Bourbon Sauce (page 263)
and/or
Mississippi Mud Pie (page 262)

America offers a rich variety of food tastes and experiences, unique to our various regions and their growing patterns and ethnic influences. In addition to these suggested menus, why not try putting together interesting menus of dishes from a combination of different parts of the country? How about Rocky Mountain Lamb (page 132) with Whipped Potato Salad (page 179)? What about Rhode Island Tuna Steaks (page 152) with Santa Fe Rice Salad (page 174)? And why not a side of Marinated Asparagus (page 207) with either? Whether you use recipes from one particular region, mix them up, or add some of your own favorites, I think you'll agree that it all adds up to a whole lot of interesting, fun, and yummy **OOH it's so GOOD!!**™

NOTE: Remember to check the yield of each recipe and adjust according to your needs.

Spice Traditions in
Regional American Cooking

New England

Maine, Vermont, New
Hampshire, Massachusetts,
Connecticut, Rhode Island

White pepper
Cinnamon
Nutmeg
Mustard
Paprika
Bay leaves

Middle Atlantic

New York, New Jersey,
Delaware, Pennsylvania,
Maryland

Black pepper
Mustard
Thyme
Parsley
Caraway
Cinnamon
Nutmeg
Allspice
Paprika

Upper South

Virginia, West Virginia,
Kentucky, North Carolina,
Tennessee

Red pepper
Black pepper
Curry powder
Filé powder
Mint
Ginger
Thyme
Sage
Mace
Nutmeg
Cinnamon
Celery Seed

Deep South

South Carolina, Georgia,
Florida, Alabama,
Mississippi, Arkansas,
Louisiana

Red pepper
Black pepper
Thyme
Sage
Parsley
Sesame seed
Celery seed
Cinnamon
Cloves
Curry powder
Paprika
Filé powder
Saffron
Garlic

Great Lakes

Ohio, Michigan, Wisconsin,
Minnesota, Illinois,
Indiana

Cinnamon
Cloves
Nutmeg
Allspice
Mustard
Cardamom
Basil
Oregano
Poppy seed
Caraway seed
Dill
Parsley
Sage
Bay leaves

Midwest

Iowa, Missouri, North
Dakota, South Dakota,
Nebraska, Kansas

Mustard
Black pepper
Caraway
Paprika
Cloves
Allspice
Thyme
Dill
Poppy seed
Turmeric
Celery seed
Cardamom

Southwest	Mountain States	Pacific Northwest
Oklahoma, Texas, New Mexico, Arizona	Colorado, Montana, Wyoming, Idaho, Utah, Nevada	Washington, Oregon
Red pepper	Cinnamon	Ginger
Garlic	Red pepper	Anise
Cinnamon	Caraway	Garlic
Oregano	Ginger	Cinnamon
Cilantro	Poppy seed	Dill
Caraway	Cardamom	
Cumin	Marjoram	
	Thyme	
	Sage	
	Rosemary	

California	Alaska	Hawaii
Red pepper	Dill	Ginger
Cilantro	Poppy seed	Cinnamon
Cumin	Caraway	Chinese 5-Spice
Ginger		Curry powder
Oregano		
Basil		
Garlic		

SOURCE: The American Spice Trade Association.

Helpful Hints

★ To make mashed potatoes light and creamy, add a small amount of the water that the potatoes were cooked in, then beat them vigorously.

★ A little lemon juice will help mask the tinny taste of canned tuna, salmon, or other canned fish.

★ Don't store onions and potatoes together. The gas given off by each causes the other to spoil more quickly.

★ To freshen French or Italian bread, hard rolls and other crusty breads, sprinkle the crust with cold water, and place the bread in a preheated 350°F. oven for 10 minutes.

★ Dipping a knife in hot water before using it will make a fresh loaf of bread easier to slice.

- ★ To cut hard-boiled eggs without breaking the yolks, first dip the knife in water.

- ★ Use a potato masher to easily chop hard-boiled eggs.

- ★ To peel boiled potatoes quickly, score lightly around the middle before cooking; afterward, simply spear the potatoes with a fork and peel the skin back from the score marks.

- ★ To make slicing an onion easier: Cut a thin slice off the top end only, pull away the papery outer skin, and slice.

- ★ To use the last bit of ketchup from a bottle, pour in some oil and vinegar and shake. It makes a delicious salad dressing.

- ★ Bring sour cream to room temperature before adding it to hot mixtures. This helps keep it from curdling. Never allow to boil.

- ★ To keep butter from burning during frying or sautéing, mix it in a 2-to-1 ratio with cooking oil.

- ★ To keep cooked, drained pasta from clumping if it's being held for later use, toss lightly with 1 tablespoon olive or other cooking oil.

- ★ To douse a small burner or oven fire, sprinkle with baking soda or salt.

- ★ Avoid marinating foods in metal containers. The acid in the marinade may ruin the container, as well as impart a metallic flavor to the marinade. Glass is best.

- ★ Honey that has become cloudy or crystallized can be made clear and smooth by placing the jar in a container of warm water and stirring the honey occasionally until the crystals dissolve. Change the warm water as necessary.

- ★ Do not add kiwifruit or fresh pineapple to gelatin salads. It prevents the gelatin from setting.

- ★ If you're cooking food on wooden skewers, soak the skewers in water for five to ten minutes before using. This will prevent the skewers from burning as the food cooks.

- ★ To ensure all items on a kabob are cooked evenly, leave at least ¼ inch between pieces of food.

- ★ When making fresh-squeezed citrus juices: To get more juice out of the fruit with the least amount of effort, press down on the fruit and roll it several times back and forth over a hard surface before cutting it in half.

Oven Tips and Temps

I get a lot of questions about oven temperature settings and placement of food items in the oven. I hope the following information answers all of *your* questions.

- ★ The temperature varies in the different areas of the oven. (It can vary as much as 25°F. from the top to the bottom!)
- ★ The oven thermostat registers its reading from the temperature in the middle of the oven.
- ★ Because heat rises, the hottest part of the oven is at the top.
- ★ The positioning of the oven shelves can affect the cooking time of the food in the oven.
- ★ Because oven thermostats are often inaccurate and tend to be unreliable at very high or low temperatures, it's a good idea to use a separate oven thermometer to check the accuracy of your oven.
- ★ When baking more than one cake in an oven that has back burners or elements, arrange the cakes side by side. If the oven has side burners, arrange the cakes back to front.
- ★ When baking cakes, leave room for the heat to circulate in the oven around baking sheets and cake pans; otherwise, the underside of the cakes will burn.

Use the following chart as a guide when a recipe is not specific about the cooking temperature.

OVEN TEMPERATURES

Below 300°F. = very slow
300°F. = slow
325°F. = moderately slow
350°F. = moderate
375°F. = moderately hot

continued

400°F.–425°F. = hot
450°F.–475°F. = very hot
500°F. or more = extremely hot

These are general guidelines that may or may not be specific to your oven. Consult your manufacturer's instructions when in doubt.

Roasting a Whole Turkey

(Nothing's More American!)

As simple as 1-2-3!

Turkey is one of today's best meat buys, both nutritionally and economically. Whole turkeys are sold oven-ready: dressed, washed, inspected, and packaged. After turkeys leave the processing plant, no hands touch them until time for kitchen preparation.

It takes only 6 minutes to prepare a defrosted whole turkey for roasting (without stuffing).

If stuffing is desired, it's often best prepared separately, placed in a covered casserole, and cooked with the turkey during the last hour of roasting time.

Follow the label instructions for roasting, or use these simple directions to obtain a beautiful golden brown, ready-to-carve-and-eat turkey:

1. **Thawing:** (If turkey is not frozen, begin with step 2.) *Do not thaw poultry at room temperature.* Leave turkey in original packaging and use one of the following methods:

   No Hurry: Place wrapped turkey on a tray in the refrigerator for 3 to 4 days; allow 5 hours per pound of turkey to completely thaw.

   Fastest: Place wrapped turkey in the sink and cover with cold water. Allow about ½ hour per pound of turkey to completely thaw. Change the water frequently.

   Refrigerate or cook the turkey when it is thawed. Refreezing uncooked turkey is not recommended.

Charts and Information

Commercially frozen *stuffed* turkeys should *not* be thawed before roasting.

2. **Preparation for Roasting:** All equipment and materials used for storage, preparation, and serving of poultry must be clean. Wash hands thoroughly with hot soapy water before and after handling raw poultry. Use hard plastic or acrylic cutting boards to prepare poultry.

   Remove the plastic wrapping from the thawed turkey. Remove the giblets and neck from the body and neck cavities. To remove the neck, it may be necessary to release the legs from the band of skin or wire fastener. Rinse the turkey inside and out with cool water, pat dry with a paper towel, and return the legs to the fastener or band of skin; or tie together loosely. Tuck the tips of the wings under the back of the turkey. The neck skin should be skewered with a poultry pin or round toothpick to the back of the turkey to provide a nice appearance for serving at the table. The turkey is now completely ready for roasting.

3. **Open Pan Roasting:** Place turkey breast-side up on a flat rack in a shallow roasting pan, about 2 inches deep. Insert the meat thermometer deep into the thickest part of the thigh next to the body, not touching the bone.

   Brush the turkey skin with vegetable oil to prevent drying. If you'd like, sprinkle with salt, pepper, paprika, and any of your favorite poultry seasonings. (I especially like to add tarragon or thyme, and garlic and onion powders.) The same flavorings will work with turkey parts, too. Turkey is done when the meat thermometer registers 180 to 185°F. and the drumstick is soft and moves easily at the joint.

   Once the skin of the turkey is golden brown, shield the breast loosely with a rectangular-shaped piece of lightweight foil to prevent overbrowning.

For bone-in parts, juices should run clear when the meat is pierced in the deepest part with a long-tined fork. Cooked turkeys should be allowed to stand for 10 to 20 minutes before carving.

Allow at least 1 to 1½ pounds of uncooked turkey per person when purchasing a whole turkey. (This allows for leftovers!)

SOURCE: The National Turkey Federation.

Charts and Information

Timetable
for Roasting a Whole Turkey (at 325°F.)

APPROXIMATE WEIGHT (IN POUNDS)	APPROXIMATE ROASTING TIME (IN HOURS)*
6 to 8	2¼ to 3¼
8 to 12	3 to 4
12 to 16	3½ to 4½
16 to 20	4 to 5
20 to 24	4½ to 5½

*Approximate Roasting Time: Factors affecting roasting times are type of oven, oven temperature, and degree of thawing. Begin checking turkey for doneness about 1 hour before end of recommended roasting time.

SOURCE: The National Turkey Federation.

Equivalents and Substitutions

Quick Measures

	EQUALS
Dash	Less than ⅛ teaspoon
3 teaspoons	1 tablespoon
4 tablespoons	¼ cup
5 tablespoons plus 1 teaspoon	⅓ cup
6 tablespoons	⅜ cup
8 tablespoons	½ cup
10 tablespoons plus 2 teaspoons	⅔ cup
12 tablespoons	¾ cup
16 tablespoons	1 cup
2 tablespoons	1 fluid ounce
1 cup	½ pint or 8 fluid ounces
2 cups	1 pint or 16 fluid ounces
4 cups	2 pints or 1 quart or 32 fluid ounces
4 quarts	1 gallon or 128 fluid ounces
2 tablespoons fat or butter	1 ounce
¼ pound (1 stick) butter	½ cup
½ pound butter	1 cup
Juice of 1 lemon	About 3 tablespoons
1 cup lemon juice	Juice of 4 to 6 lemons
Juice of 1 orange	About ½ cup
Grated peel of 1 lemon	About 1½ teaspoons
Grated peel of 1 orange	About 1 tablespoon

1 POUND* OF	EQUALS APPROXIMATELY
Flour	4 cups
Cornmeal	3 cups

*One pound equals 16 ounces avoirdupois (our usual standard of weight measurement).

continued

Cornstarch	3 cups
Granulated sugar	2 cups
Brown sugar	3 cups
Confectioners' sugar	3½ cups
Raisins	3 cups
Rice	2 cups
Macaroni	4 cups
Meat	2 cups, chopped
Diced cooked chicken	3 cups
Potatoes	2 cups, diced, or 3 to 4 medium potatoes
Chopped onions	3 cups
Cheese	4 cups, grated
Bananas	3 medium
Ground coffee	3½ cups

Substitutions

INSTEAD OF:	USE:
1 cup canned tomatoes	1⅓ cups chopped fresh tomatoes, simmered for 10 minutes
½ pound fresh mushrooms	1 can or jar (4 ounces) mushroom pieces
1 teaspoon Worcestershire sauce	1 teaspoon bottled steak sauce
Few drops hot pepper sauce	Dash of cayenne or crushed red pepper
1 cup canned beef bouillon	1 beef bouillon cube or 1 envelope instant beef broth dissolved in 1 cup boiling water
1 cup canned chicken broth	1 chicken bouillon cube or 1 envelope instant chicken broth dissolved in 1 cup boiling water
1 cup beef or chicken stock	1 cup canned beef or chicken broth

1 cup milk	½ cup evaporated milk plus ½ cup water or 4 tablespoons powdered milk plus 1 cup water
1 teaspoon Italian seasoning	¼ teaspoon each dried oregano, basil, thyme, and rosemary, plus dash of cayenne pepper
1 tablespoon dehydrated minced onion	¼ cup finely minced fresh onion
1 teaspoon onion powder	1 medium-sized onion
⅛ teaspoon garlic powder	1 garlic clove
1 tablespoon dehydrated parsley flakes	3 tablespoons fresh minced parsley
1 teaspoon pumpkin pie spice	½ teaspoon ground cinnamon, ¼ teaspoon ground ginger, and ⅛ teaspoon each ground nutmeg and ground cloves
¼ cup cinnamon sugar	¼ cup granulated sugar plus 1 teaspoon ground cinnamon
1 teaspoon allspice	½ teaspoon ground cinnamon plus ⅛ teaspoon ground cloves
1½ cups corn syrup	1 cup sugar plus ½ cup water
1 tablespoon cornstarch	2 tablespoons flour (for thickening purposes)
1 teaspoon baking powder	¼ teaspoon baking soda plus ½ teaspoon cream of tartar
1 ounce chocolate	1 square or ¼ cup cocoa plus ½ tablespoon shortening

Packaged Foods Note

As with many processed foods, package sizes may vary by brand. Generally, the sizes indicated in these recipes are average sizes. If you can't find the exact indicated package size, whatever package is closest in size will usually do the trick.

Bean Bread Spread

8 to 10 servings
(about 1¼ cups)

Try whipping up this one and you'll be doing some
California dreamin' before you know it!

1 loaf Italian bread
½ cup olive oil, plus extra for brushing on bread
1 can (15 to 16 ounces) garbanzo beans (chick peas), drained
3 to 5 garlic cloves, coarsely chopped (to taste)

1 tablespoon fresh lemon juice
1 teaspoon salt
1 teaspoon pepper
½ teaspoon chili powder
¼ cup coarsely chopped fresh parsley for garnish

Preheat the oven to 375°F. Slice the bread in half lengthwise, brush the cut side of each half with olive oil, and bake for about 20 minutes or until golden brown. Meanwhile, in a blender jar, place the ½ cup olive oil, garbanzo beans, garlic, lemon juice, salt, pepper, and chili powder, in that order. (It will blend better.) Purée, mixing frequently, until it becomes a paste. Spread the paste on the bread, garnish with the parsley, and slice into serving-sized pieces.

Buffalo Chicken Wings

40 to 50 wings
(2½ cups sauce)

*We don't have to "shuffle off to Buffalo" to get the real thing—we
can make authentic wings right in our own kitchen. And it's
so easy, 'cause instead of deep-frying them (which is
the way the restaurants do it), we crisp them in
the oven. (Oh, and let's not forget to give the folks
in Youngstown, Ohio, and Sharon, Pennsylvania,
credit for their great wings, too!)*

10 pounds chicken wings
(thawed, if frozen)

SAUCE
1   cup (2 sticks) butter
1½ cups cayenne pepper sauce

Preheat the oven to 425°F. Split the wings at each joint and discard the tips; rinse, then pat dry. Place the wings on cookie sheets and bake for 30 minutes. Turn the wings and bake for an additional 30 minutes, until brown. Drain well and place in a large bowl. In a small saucepan, melt the butter over medium-low heat. Turn off the heat and stir in the hot pepper sauce; toss with the cooked chicken wings. Keep warm until ready to serve.

NOTE: Try serving the wings with blue cheese dressing and celery sticks for the genuine Buffalo wing experience! And you can bake the wings ahead of time and store them in the fridge or freezer; then, before serving, simply warm them in the oven and toss them with the sauce.

California Spinach Appetizers

60 to 70 balls

*I'm no historian, but maybe, just maybe, Horace Greeley said
"Go west, young man!" because he knew
the food was gonna be great!*

2 packages (10 ounces each)
   frozen chopped spinach,
   thawed, drained, and
   squeezed dry
1½ cups grated Parmesan
   cheese
⅔ cup seasoned bread crumbs

6 eggs, beaten
½ cup (1 stick) butter, melted
1 cup chopped onion
1 teaspoon dried oregano
½ teaspoon garlic powder

Preheat the oven to 350°F. In a large bowl, mix together all the ingredients. Shape the mixture into golf ball–sized balls and place on cookie sheets that have been coated with nonstick vegetable spray. Bake for 20 to 25 minutes or until the balls start to turn golden.

Cheesy Crab Dip

12 servings

Ooh, very classy! Ooh, very easy!
Ooh, very Chesapeake tasty!

12 ounces cream cheese, softened
1 cup (½ pint) sour cream
1¼ cups shredded Cheddar cheese, divided
2 tablespoons mayonnaise
1 tablespoon seafood seasoning
1 tablespoon lemon juice
1 teaspoon prepared mustard
1 teaspoon Worcestershire sauce
Garlic powder to taste
1 pound canned crabmeat

Preheat the oven to 375°F. In a large bowl, mix together all the ingredients except crabmeat and ¼ cup Cheddar cheese. Fold in the crabmeat. Put the mixture in a 1½-quart casserole dish that has been coated with nonstick vegetable spray. Bake for 20 minutes. Sprinkle the top with the remaining ¼ cup Cheddar cheese and bake for 5 minutes more.

NOTE: Serve with an assortment of crackers. You can use imitation crabmeat instead of the canned, and any mellow cheese instead of the Cheddar—whatever works best for you!

Chicken & Chips

18 to 20 pieces

Here's an American-style spinoff on the traditional English fish and chips that carried over first to New England and spread from there to the whole country. And now that chicken has become the big "WOW!," wait till you see what happens when you serve this—it'll be an "everybody loves it" favorite.

⅓ cup milk	¼ teaspoon pepper
1 egg	1½ chicken breasts, skinned, boned, and cut into 1-inch pieces
1¼ cups (1 6-ounce bag) sour-cream-and-onion-flavored potato chips, finely crushed	2 tablespoons butter, melted
¼ teaspoon onion powder	

Preheat the oven to 400°F. In a small bowl, beat together the milk and egg with a fork until well mixed. In a shallow dish, combine the crushed potato chips, onion powder, and pepper. Dip the chicken pieces into the egg mixture, then roll them in the potato chip mixture. Repeat until all the chicken is coated. Arrange the coated pieces in a single layer in a baking pan that has been coated with nonstick vegetable spray. Let sit at room temperature for 15 minutes, then drizzle the chicken with the melted butter. Bake for 10 to 15 minutes, or until firm and golden brown.

NOTE: Serve with ranch dressing as a dipping sauce, or use your favorite potato chip dip.

Confetti Bites

about 18 servings

*Like the stars in the Northwest that look like shining confetti,
here's a colorful delight that's sure to please the whole gang!
(And we get a head start with packaged crescent rolls.)*

2 packages (8 ounces each) refrigerator crescent rolls

2 packages (8 ounces each) cream cheese, softened

3 tablespoons mayonnaise

½ teaspoon dried basil

¼ teaspoon garlic powder

3 cups finely chopped fresh vegetables (cucumbers, tomatoes, broccoli, bell peppers, or any colorful combination of your favorites)

Preheat the oven to 350°F. Press the crescent roll dough onto a 10" × 15" cookie sheet to form a crust. Bake for 10 to 15 minutes or until light golden, then allow to cool. Meanwhile, in a medium-sized bowl, combine the cream cheese, mayonnaise, basil, and garlic powder. Spread the mixture thinly over the cooled crust. Top with the chopped vegetables. Cut and serve.

NOTE: It cuts best with a pizza cutter.

Deviled Eggs

24 servings

These are such an American standard that they may have been here before the Pilgrims . . . so here's the easiest and tastiest way to be oh, so devilish.

12 hard-boiled eggs

2 tablespoons bottled French dressing

2 tablespoons sour cream

¼ teaspoon salt

¼ teaspoon pepper

1 tablespoon ketchup

¾ teaspoon mustard powder

2 dashes Worcestershire sauce

Paprika for sprinkling

Carefully peel the eggs and cut them in half lengthwise; remove the yolks and place them in a large bowl. Set aside the egg whites. Mash the yolks with a fork; blend in the French dressing and sour cream. Mix in the salt, pepper, ketchup, mustard, and Worcestershire sauce. Carefully place the mixture back in the egg whites and sprinkle with the paprika. For best results, refrigerate until ½ hour before serving.

Full-of-Beans Dip

10 to 12 servings

*Talk about a Southwestern taste explosion—just put this
out with tortilla chips and stand back!*

2 cans (9 ounces each) jalapeño
bean dip
1 package (8 ounces) cream
cheese, softened
1 cup sour cream
½ cup finely chopped onion

Hot pepper sauce to taste
(optional)
2 cups grated Cheddar or
Monterey Jack cheese,
divided

Preheat the oven to 350°F. In a large bowl, mix together all the
ingredients, except the Cheddar cheese. Add 1½ cups of the Cheddar cheese; mix again gently. Place the mixture in an 8-inch-square
glass baking dish that has been coated with nonstick vegetable
spray; sprinkle the top with the remaining ½ cup Cheddar cheese.
Bake for 15 to 20 minutes or until the cheese melts and the dip is
warmed through.

Garden Squares

15 servings
(or 6 to 8 side-dish servings)

*Zucchini's such a summer garden favorite that we should
designate it our national vegetable. Here's another easy way
to fix it that I first had on a Rhode Island beach—but
it's really a great all-over-the-U.S. treat for a
whole gang. (So inexpensive, too!)*

4   eggs, beaten
½ cup grated Parmesan cheese
½ cup chopped onion
½ teaspoon seasoned salt
½ teaspoon dried oregano
½ teaspoon garlic powder
¼ cup chopped fresh parsley or
    2 tablespoons dried parsley
    flakes
½ cup vegetable oil

½ cup whole wheat flour
1   cup biscuit baking mix
1   cup grated yellow squash
    (about ½ of a medium-sized
    squash)
1   cup grated zucchini (about ½
    of a small zucchini)
1   cup peeled, grated carrots
    (about 2 medium-sized
    carrots)

Preheat the oven to 375°F. In a large bowl, mix together all the
ingredients. Pour the mixture into an ungreased 9-inch-square baking dish and bake for 30 to 35 minutes or until firm, and the edges
are light golden. Cool for a few minutes, then cut into squares.

NOTE: If you have the time, give it a zip with chopped fresh garlic instead of garlic powder.

Glazed Macadamia Chicken Wings

16 to 20 wings

*How 'bout this "sweet" idea for chicken wings
with a Hawaiian flair?*

4 pounds chicken wings	1 tablespoon soy sauce
1 cup orange marmalade	¼ cup molasses
¼ cup honey	⅛ teaspoon cayenne pepper
½ cup chopped macadamia nuts	

Preheat the oven to 350°F. Split the wings at each joint and discard the tips; rinse, then pat dry. Place the wings in a greased and foil-lined shallow baking pan and bake for 15 minutes. Meanwhile, in a small saucepan, combine the remaining ingredients; cook, stirring, over a low heat until the marmalade melts, about 2 minutes. Brush the marmalade mixture over the chicken wings; continue to bake until the chicken is cooked through, about 20 minutes more, basting and turning occasionally. Finish off the wings by broiling them for 2 to 3 minutes per side, or until golden brown. Serve topped with the pan juices.

NOTE: The more basting you do while the wings are cooking, the better the flavor. And they're best made ahead and reheated just before serving. Don't have macadamias?? Almonds will work well, also.

Honey-Dijon Chicken Wings

40 to 50 wings
(3 cups sauce)

Who says we've always got to stick with traditional chicken wings?
Here's a "honey" of a taste twist! (It's basically those
Buffalo wings—but with a little something special.)

10 pounds chicken wings (thawed, if frozen)	SAUCE
	¾ cup cayenne pepper sauce
	1 cup Dijon-style mustard or other prepared mustard
	1½ cups honey

Preheat the oven to 425°F. Split the wings at each joint and discard the tips; rinse, then pat dry. Place the wings on cookie sheets and bake for 30 minutes. Turn the wings and bake for an additional 30 minutes, until brown. Drain well and place in a large bowl. In a small saucepan, combine all the sauce ingredients. Mix well, then heat the mixture over medium heat for 2 to 3 minutes, or until the honey dissolves. Remove from heat and toss with the cooked chicken wings. Keep warm until ready to serve.

NOTE: You can bake the wings ahead of time and store them in the fridge or freezer; then, before serving, simply warm them in the oven and toss them with the sauce. It couldn't be easier!

Hot Artichoke Spread

about 1 quart

Taste the best of California . . . I promise it's unexpectedly tasty
(and a favorite at almost all of my own parties)!

1 cup mayonnaise

2 cans (14 ounces each) artichoke hearts (water packed, not marinated), drained, or 2 packages (9 ounces each) frozen artichoke hearts, thawed

1 drop hot pepper sauce

1 small garlic clove, minced

1 teaspoon lemon juice

1 cup grated Parmesan cheese

Preheat the oven to 350°F. Place all the ingredients in a food processor and blend until smooth. (If using a blender instead of a food processor, stop the machine frequently and scrape down the sides of the container with a rubber spatula, after the blades have stopped completely. Blend just until the mixture is smooth.) Coat a 1½-quart baking dish with nonstick vegetable spray, then pour in the mixture. Bake for 30 minutes, or until lightly browned.

NOTE: Serve on cocktail rye bread. You can also bake this spread in several small baking dishes. When cool, cover each with plastic wrap and freeze for later use. When ready to use, thaw, then remove plastic wrap, and rewarm in the oven or microwave.

Maryland Crabmeat Spread

about 1½ cups

*When we think of Maryland, our taste buds naturally
yearn for crabmeat. This one **won't** disappoint!*

½ teaspoon Worcestershire
  sauce
1 can (8 ounces) crabmeat,
  drained
1 tablespoon lemon juice
1 scallion, finely chopped
1 package (8 ounces) cream
  cheese

⅛ teaspoon salt
4 teaspoons milk
Dash of hot pepper sauce
1 teaspoon seafood seasoning
1 teaspoon dried dillweed

In a large, microwaveable bowl, mix together all the ingredients.
Microwave on high for 2 minutes; stir. Microwave for an additional
2 minutes. Cover and refrigerate.

NOTE: Serve with your favorite crackers or chips.

New England Clam Spread

12 to 18 servings

*Here's a quick dip that's bound to make your guests hear
oceans and marshes nearby, 'cause from Connecticut to Maine
(and beyond) clams mean "seashore"!*

1 can (6½ ounces) minced clams, undrained

1 can (10½ ounces) white clam sauce

1 strip (4 ounces) saltine crackers, crumbled

4 drops hot pepper sauce

½ teaspoon dried oregano

1 medium-sized onion, chopped

6 tablespoons (¾ stick) butter

Preheat the oven to 350°F. In a large bowl, mix together all the ingredients except the onion and butter; set aside. In a large skillet over medium heat, sauté the onion in the butter until transparent. Stir the sautéed onion into the clam mixture. Place the mixture in a 1-quart baking dish that has been coated with nonstick vegetable spray. Bake for 20 to 30 minutes or until light golden.

NOTE: Serve warm as a spread with crackers or cocktail bread.

Pesto Cheesecake Appetizer

10 to 12 servings

Attention, basil lovers: Here's one I'll bet you haven't
tried yet. This unlikely combination of flavors is
an exciting trip to the herb garden.

1 tablespoon olive oil
1 cup fresh basil leaves
¼ teaspoon salt
1 garlic clove
1 package (8 ounces) cream cheese, softened

½ cup ricotta cheese
2 eggs
¼ cup grated Parmesan cheese
1 prepared 9-inch butter-flavored pie crust
¼ cup sliced almonds

Preheat the oven to 350°F. Purée the olive oil, basil, salt, and garlic in a food processor or blender; set aside. In a large bowl, combine the cream cheese and ricotta cheese; blend well with an electric mixer on high speed. Add the eggs, one at a time, beating well with an electric mixer on high after each addition. Stir in the Parmesan cheese. Mix in the basil mixture and pour into the crust. Sprinkle with the sliced almonds. Bake for 35 to 45 minutes or until a knife inserted into the center comes out clean. Allow to cool to room temperature and serve.

NOTE: This is a unique dish that's especially good when you use home-grown or farmers' market fresh basil.

Salmon Mousse

18 to 25 servings

You'll be the hit of any party with this Northwestern taste delight. This was one of our most requested dishes when my wife and I were caterers. (No, no, it's not difficult at all!)

1 envelope (.25 ounces) unflavored gelatin
1 cup water
½ teaspoon salt
4 tablespoons sugar
2 tablespoons lemon juice
3 tablespoons white vinegar
2 teaspoons red horseradish

2 teaspoons grated onion
1 can (15½ ounces) pink or red salmon, drained and flaked
1 large stalk celery, finely chopped
6 pitted black olives, finely chopped
½ cup mayonnaise

In a medium-sized saucepan, mix the gelatin with the water; dissolve over low heat. Remove from heat, then add the salt, sugar, lemon juice, vinegar, horseradish, and onion. In a large bowl, mix together the salmon, celery, olives, and mayonnaise. Add the slightly cooled gelatin mixture, then pour into a 4-cup decorative mold and chill until set, about 2 hours.

NOTE: Invert and unmold onto a serving platter. Serve on crackers or sliced cocktail rye bread.

Sausage Roll-Ups

16 roll-ups

*Here's an easy Tennessee-inspired dish for unexpected company—
and be sure to make lots, 'cause these disappear almost
as fast as you can make them!*

2 packages (8 ounces each)
refrigerator crescent rolls
(16 rolls)

1 package (8 ounces) brown 'n'
serve sausages (8 sausages)

6 thin slices Swiss cheese

Preheat the oven to 375°F. Separate the crescent rolls into triangles. Cut each sausage in half; cut the cheese slices into thirds. Wrap each sausage half in a piece of cheese (you'll have two extras), then in a crescent roll, overlapping ends and sealing completely. Place on an ungreased cookie sheet and bake until golden brown, 12 to 15 minutes.

NOTE: Try using 1 package (8 ounces) of cocktail franks instead of sausage (they don't have to be cut in half). And for a bit more snap, try adding a dab of mustard on each one before wrapping in the crescent roll!

Southwestern Dip

3½ cups

They sure know how to make a tasty dip in the Southwest.
*(In fact, they know how to make **everything** tasty*
in the Southwest.) Try it . . . it's got real zip!

2 packages (8 ounces each) cream cheese, softened

½ cup sour cream

1 jar (8 ounces) mild or medium salsa

1 teaspoon seasoned salt

In medium-sized bowl, beat the cream cheese until smooth. Stir in the sour cream. Fold in the salsa and seasoned salt. Serve at room temperature. Store, covered, in the refrigerator.

NOTE: Enjoy with chips or veggies.

Tortilla Cheese Roll-Ups

10 roll-ups

*Here's a really easy, fun way to enjoy a taste of the Southwest.
And instead of salsa, you can add anything from peanut
butter to ham and mustard, chopped cooked bacon, or
apple slices! Why not make an assortment for
some quick entertaining?*

1 package (10 ounces) 7-inch
flour tortillas (10 shells)

10 pieces string cheese
1 jar (8 ounces) salsa

Place 1 piece of the string cheese in each tortilla; top each piece of cheese with 1 tablespoon of salsa and roll up the tortillas. Place the rolls, seam-side down, on a microwaveable plate. Pop them into the microwave, a few at a time, and heat for 20 to 30 seconds, or until the cheese starts to melt. Let the rolls cool a bit before serving.

NOTE: You can prepare the roll-ups in advance, store them in the refrigerator, and then just microwave them when you're ready to serve.

Western Chicken Wings

40 to 50 wings
(2¼ cups sauce)

*Wings that smack of barbecue flavor—a treat we can easily
whip up from our chuckwagon, pardner! What it does is
team easy wing cooking with today's popular taste.*

10 pounds chicken wings
    (thawed, if frozen)

SAUCE

2 cups mild barbecue sauce

¼ cup prepared mustard

2 tablespoons cayenne pepper
   sauce

4½ teaspoons garlic powder

Preheat the oven to 425°F. Split the wings at each joint and discard the tips; rinse, then pat dry. Place the wings on cookie sheets
and bake for 30 minutes. Turn the wings and bake for an additional
30 minutes, or until brown. Drain well and place in a large bowl.
Combine all the sauce ingredients in a medium-sized bowl. Mix
well, then toss with the cooked chicken wings. Keep warm until
ready to serve.

NOTE: You can bake the wings ahead of time and store them in the
fridge or freezer; then, before serving, simply warm them in the oven
and toss them with the sauce.

Relishes, Sauces, and Dressings

August Corn Relish

about 2½ cups

Don't know what to do with those few leftover ears of summer corn? Turn them into a Southwestern-type relish. Well, you know how everybody goes nuts for those fresh, homestyle touches!

Kernels from 3 ears of cooked corn or 1 can (15 to 17 ounces) whole-kernel corn, drained

⅓ cup sweet 'n' spicy French dressing

1 carrot, finely diced

⅓ cup chopped green bell pepper

¼ cup chopped onion

2 tablespoons pickle relish

2 tablespoons chopped pimiento

½ teaspoon celery seed

In a medium-sized bowl, combine all the ingredients and mix well. Cover and chill for 24 hours.

NOTE: For a variation, try adding ½ teaspoon of mustard seed. Or leave out the pickle relish and add ½ teaspoon of sugar and 1 minced clove of garlic.

Continental Steak Sauce

about ½ cup

American beef teams so naturally with this simple treat.
Just the aroma makes me ravenous! And have you
noticed that beef (steak, in particular) is
coming back stronger than ever? There's
a reason we love it . . . mmm!

4 tablespoons (½ stick) butter
1 garlic clove, crushed
4 scallions, chopped
1 tablespoon Dijon-style
  mustard

1 tablespoon dry white wine
1 teaspoon Worcestershire
  sauce

In a small skillet over medium heat, sauté the garlic and scallions in the butter for about 1 minute. While stirring continuously, mix in the remaining ingredients.

NOTE: Drizzle this sauce over cooked steak slices.

Cranberry Relish

about 3 cups

Originally, we got fresh cranberries only when they were harvested from the Massachusetts bogs. Now we can enjoy the taste of cranberries all year-round. (I like this so much better than cooked cranberry sauce that it has become not only our Thanksgiving favorite but our go-with-any-type-of-roast favorite.)

1 apple, cored and cut into quarters (with skin on)

1 small seedless orange, cut into quarters (with skin on)

1 bag (12 ounces) cranberries (fresh or frozen)

¾ cup sugar (or to taste)

Place the apple and orange in a food processor and finely chop. Add the cranberries and continue processing until the mixture is finely chopped. Transfer to a bowl and add the sugar, mixing well.

Cucumber Dill Dip

about 3½ cups

*I love these Pennsylvania Dutch flavors anytime, but
I especially like to mix this up when my garden
is full of fresh cucumbers and dill!*

1 cup mayonnaise

1 cup sour cream

1 package (8 ounces) cream
cheese, softened

1 medium-sized cucumber,
peeled, seeded, and chopped

1 tablespoon chopped fresh
parsley

1 cup chopped scallions

1 tablespoon fresh lemon juice

1 tablespoon finely chopped
fresh dill or ½ teaspoon dried
dillweed

¼ teaspoon salt

¼ teaspoon white pepper

Place all the ingredients in a food processor or an electric blender; process until almost smooth. Pour into a bowl, cover, and chill for 2 hours to "marry" the flavors.

NOTE: Serve with veggies, crackers, tacos, or chips, or use as a salad dressing.

Deep Southern Hot Barbecue Sauce

about 2¼ cups

*One of my favorite things about the South is its great barbecues.
So here's a bit of authentic barbecue that you can whip up
right in your own kitchen. (Maybe not exactly like at
Kilgore, Texas's Country Tavern, but for
homemade . . . it sure is easy.)*

2 teaspoons vegetable oil	2 tablespoons white vinegar
⅓ cup minced onion	⅓ cup firmly packed dark brown sugar
1 garlic clove, minced	
1 cup chicken broth or bouillon	2 tablespoons parsley flakes
1 can (8 ounces) tomato sauce	¼ teaspoon salt
1 can (6 ounces) tomato paste	¼ teaspoon cayenne pepper

In a medium-sized saucepan, heat the oil over medium-high heat. Add the onion and garlic; sauté for 4 minutes or until golden. Remove from heat, then add the remaining ingredients. Reduce heat to low and simmer, uncovered, for 15 minutes, stirring occasionally. Store in the refrigerator for up to 1 week.

NOTE: Use as a basting sauce for chicken, pork, fish, or beef.

Dill Dip

about 2 cups

With a dilly of a fresh taste like this, they'll dip till it's
all gone! And check out the note at the bottom . . .
that makes it a "double dip"!

1 cup mayonnaise	½ teaspoon salt
1 cup (½ pint) sour cream	½ teaspoon pepper
½ cup chopped fresh parsley	½ cup chopped fresh dill or 3 to
¼ cup finely chopped onion	4 tablespoons dried dillweed
2 tablespoons fresh lemon juice	

In a large bowl, combine all the ingredients; mix well and chill, covered, for at least 2 hours before serving.

NOTE: All you have to do is add ½ to ¾ cup of milk to this recipe and you've got a fresh garden salad dressing.

Fresh Salsa

about 4 cups

Wow!! No wonder everybody is wild for Tex-Mex—
it's so satisfying and full-flavored!

3 tomatoes, finely chopped

1 small onion, finely chopped

½ teaspoon salt

1 tablespoon lime or lemon juice

1 jalapeño pepper, finely chopped

2 tablespoons finely chopped parsley

1 garlic clove, finely chopped

1 teaspoon vegetable oil

1 can (8 ounces) tomato sauce (about ⅞ cup)

Dash of hot pepper sauce

Combine all the ingredients in a medium-sized bowl; mix well. Cover and chill for at least 2 hours to blend the flavors. Serve at room temperature.

NOTE: If you'd like a thicker salsa, strain the mixture before serving.

Fresh Tomato Dip

about 2 cups

Yet another way to use those fresh-from-the-vine tomatoes—mmm!

1½ packages (12 ounces) cream cheese, softened at room temperature

¼ cup mayonnaise

1 ripe tomato, cut into quarters

2 tablespoons chopped onion

2 garlic cloves

1 celery stalk, cut into chunks

2 tablespoons fresh lemon or lime juice

1 teaspoon sugar

½ teaspoon salt

3 to 4 drops hot pepper sauce, or to taste

Combine all the ingredients in a blender or food processor. Blend until smooth. Remove the dip to a serving bowl; cover and chill.

NOTE: Serve with your favorite veggies, crackers, or crunchies. This makes a good base for other dips, too. For a Spanish flavor add chopped olives, for French add tarragon, for Italian add basil, and for Tex-Mex add chili powder. If you use less cream cheese it can be a super fresh tomato salad dressing.

Garlic Mayonnaise

about 1 cup

I call this "mayonnaise with just the right zest"!

3 garlic cloves, peeled
1 egg
1 tablespoon lemon juice or
   white wine vinegar

½ teaspoon salt
1 cup olive oil

Place the garlic, egg, lemon juice, and salt in a blender; blend until smooth. Continue blending, slowly adding the oil to the blender; blend until the mixture thickens like mayonnaise. As with any dish containing raw eggs, be sure to store it in the refrigerator until ready to use.

NOTE: If you have any concerns about using a recipe containing raw eggs, then skip this one.

Joe's Stone Crab Mustard Sauce

about 1 cup

Not only is this perfect for dipping stone crabs, but any fish or seafood can be made richer with it! This recipe came from my friends at Joe's Stone Crab Restaurant in South Miami Beach. The restaurant is a Miami classic, an institution—a must for every tourist and every South Florida local!

1 tablespoon plus ½ teaspoon mustard powder, or more to taste

1 cup mayonnaise

2 teaspoons Worcestershire sauce

1 teaspoon steak sauce

2 tablespoons heavy cream

2 tablespoons milk

Pinch of salt

In a medium-sized bowl, combine the mustard powder and mayonnaise; beat for 1 minute with an electric beater. Add the remaining ingredients and beat until the mixture is well blended and creamy. Cover and chill until ready to serve.

NOTE: If you'd like a little more mustardy bite, whisk about ½ teaspoon more mustard powder into the finished sauce until well blended.

New York Pushcart Onion Sauce

about 2 cups
(enough for 6 to 8 hot dogs)

*You've gotta admit that some of the greatest food originated in
New York. Like, here's the sauce that all the pushcart
vendors have for drizzling over their hot dogs. It's
a New York tradition. And for us at home . . .
no more plain old hot dogs!*

2 tablespoons vegetable oil
2 medium-sized onions, cut into
   ¼-inch slices
¼ cup ketchup
Pinch of ground cinnamon

⅛ teaspoon chili powder
Dash of hot pepper sauce
Dash of salt
1 cup water

In a medium-sized skillet, heat the oil over medium heat; add
the onions and sauté until golden and limp, about 7 minutes. Mix
in the ketchup, then add the cinnamon, chili powder, hot pepper
sauce, and salt. Pour in the water and stir. Bring the mixture to a
boil, reduce heat, and simmer, uncovered, for about 10 minutes or
until the mixture is heated through.

NOTE: This is really great spooned over cooked hot dogs, but try it with
other foods, too, and watch how fast they disappear!

Special Mayonnaises

Here's a Northwest fresh herb touch that'll make you a culinary whiz. Try a different one each time. Why, you might not want plain mayonnaise ever again!

Herb Mayonnaise

1 cup

1 cup real or light mayonnaise
1 tablespoon dried dillweed (or 2 tablespoons chopped fresh dillweed)

1 tablespoon parsley flakes (or 2 tablespoons chopped fresh parsley)
1 tablespoon fresh lemon juice

Combine all the ingredients in a small bowl. Cover; chill to blend the flavors. Store in the refrigerator, covered, for up to 1 week.

NOTE: Serve with grilled or roasted meats, poultry, seafood, or vegetables.

Horseradish Mayonnaise

1¼ cups

1 cup real or light mayonnaise
⅓ cup prepared horseradish

½ teaspoon Worcestershire sauce

Prepare as above. Store in the refrigerator, covered, for up to 2 weeks.

NOTE: Serve with roast beef, or grilled or smoked meats.

Pesto Mayonnaise

1¼ cups

1 cup real or light mayonnaise   ¼ cup prepared pesto sauce

Prepare as above. Store in the refrigerator, covered, for up to 1 week.

NOTE: Serve with roast beef, or grilled meats, poultry, seafood, or vegetables.

Spinach Salad Dressing

about 1¼ cups

*Those sun-loving folks in California love salad and this
dressing is a big favorite. (I'm not from California,
but it happens to be one of my favorites, too!)*

1 bottle (8 ounces) Italian salad
   dressing

¼ cup sugar
Dash of hot pepper sauce

In a small saucepan, combine all the ingredients; heat over low heat until the sugar has dissolved. Use immediately or store the unused dressing, covered, in the refrigerator. Simply reheat when ready to use.

NOTE: This is especially good served warm over a salad of fresh spinach leaves, mushrooms, hard-boiled eggs, and bacon (or bacon bits). Always put your dressing on at the last minute so the spinach stays crispy.

Tartar Sauce

1½ cups

This sauce can be a real spark for almost any fish dish,
and it can make a fish lover out of almost anyone!
Yes, it may have started in the Northeast,
but you'd never know it now . . .
it's everywhere.

6 tablespoons pickle relish

2 tablespoons onion powder

1 cup mayonnaise

1 tablespoon chopped fresh parsley

2 teaspoons chopped pimiento-stuffed green olives

Combine all the ingredients in a medium-sized bowl. Cover and chill until ready to use.

Tasty Apricot Barbecue Sauce

about 3 cups

Want them to thank you for exciting the barbecue with something more than the "plain old regular"? Well, this is the Fourth of July of sauces!!

1   can (10½ ounces) condensed tomato soup

½   cup dark brown sugar

1   jar (10 to 12 ounces) apricot preserves (about 1 cup)

½   cup bottled Italian dressing

1   tablespoon dried onion flakes or 3 tablespoons finely chopped fresh onion

1   teaspoon garlic salt (or ¾ teaspoon salt plus ¼ teaspoon garlic powder)

½   teaspoon pepper

1   teaspoon Worcestershire sauce

2   tablespoons apple cider vinegar

Place all the ingredients in a medium-sized saucepan. Heat over medium heat, stirring occasionally, until the preserves melt and the mixture is heated through, about 5 minutes.

NOTE: Use as a dipping sauce for barbecued foods or add some of this sauce to your grilled items during the last five minutes of cooking, pouring any extra over the top before serving.

West Coast Seafood Dressing

2½ cups

*Even though this is the ideal dressing for chilled seafood like
shrimp, crabmeat, or imitation crabmeat, you're gonna find
even more ways to enjoy it. Okay, finally the truth
comes out . . . this is what I use now when I
make Russian dressing for myself.*

1 cup mayonnaise	2 tablespoons chopped pimiento-stuffed green olives
¼ cup sour cream	⅛ teaspoon salt
½ cup red chili sauce	⅛ teaspoon pepper
2 hard-boiled eggs, chopped	
¼ cup finely chopped scallions or onion	

Mix together all the ingredients in a medium-sized bowl. Store
in the refrigerator until ready to use.

White Raisin Sauce

1½ cups

This might be Pennsylvania Dutch, or it might be pure Midwest . . .
it's a toss-up. But one thing I know, it's perfect as
a ham glaze or for adding a touch
of elegance to any meal.

1 cup white raisins	Dash of salt
1 cup sugar	⅛ teaspoon pepper
½ cup water	¼ cup currant or seedless
2 tablespoons butter	raspberry jelly

In a medium-sized saucepan, combine the raisins, sugar, and water; heat over medium-low heat until warm and blended, about 5 minutes. Add the butter, salt, and pepper; heat until well blended. Mix in the jelly just until warmed through.

NOTE: Pour this sauce over a 5-pound canned ham and bake at 325°F. for 1 hour. Serve the glaze from the pan over the ham slices and WOW!!

Soups and Chowders

Beans 'n' Franks Chowder

4 servings
(about 5 cups)

*The Scandinavian and German heritages of the Midwest may
each lay claim to this, but on a chilly night when you want
something hearty in a jiffy . . . all you really need to
know is "thick, rich, and tasty" says it all! This'll
warm your tummy, all right.*

2 cans (16 ounces each) baked beans, divided

4 hot dogs, cut into ½-inch pieces

¼ cup chopped onion

2 tablespoons (¼ stick) butter

1 can (14 ounces) whole tomatoes, broken up, undrained

1 tablespoon brown sugar

¼ teaspoon hot pepper sauce

Set aside 1 cup of the baked beans. In a large bowl, mash the remaining beans or purée in a blender; set aside. In a large saucepan over medium-high heat, sauté the hot dog pieces and onion in the butter for 3 to 5 minutes, or until lightly browned. Add the undrained tomatoes, brown sugar, and hot pepper sauce. Simmer for 10 minutes. Add the 1 cup reserved beans and puréed beans; cook slowly for 10 to 15 minutes, stirring occasionally, until the soup is piping hot.

NOTE: This is easy and so thick—just great for dipping with crusty bread or toasted hot dog buns!

Cape Cod Wharf Soup

about 12 cups

Ahhh! Summer on Cape Cod! There's nothing like it . . .
and now you can re-create it anytime.

1   medium-sized onion, diced
3   to 4 celery stalks, diced
2   medium-sized green bell
    peppers, diced
½ cup (1 stick) butter
2   medium-sized potatoes,
    peeled and diced
5   cups canned tomatoes,
    broken up, undrained (about
    3 14½-ounce cans)

6   cups chicken broth
½   teaspoon salt
½   teaspoon black pepper
1½ pounds fish, cut into 1-inch
    pieces (cod, haddock,
    flounder, or any other white-
    fleshed fish)

In a soup pot over medium heat, sauté the onion, celery, and green pepper in the butter until tender. Add the potatoes, tomatoes, and chicken broth. Bring to a boil, then reduce the heat and simmer for 20 minutes. Add the remaining ingredients and cook for 10 minutes more.

NOTE: If you're like me and you like a thicker style of soup, stir in ½ cup of instant mashed potatoes when you add the fish.

Corn and Potato Chowder

7 cups

Here's a farm-style chowder that's full of
American heartland richness.

1 cup chopped onion (about ½ of a medium-sized onion)

2 garlic cloves, peeled and thinly sliced

1 tablespoon butter

2 cups diced potatoes (about 1 large potato)

1 cup chopped red or green bell pepper (about 1 medium-sized pepper)

2 cups chicken broth

¼ teaspoon ground black pepper

¼ teaspoon ground marjoram

1 large or 2 small bay leaves

Dash nutmeg (optional)

1 can (16½ ounces) cream-style corn

1 can (7 ounces) whole-kernel corn, drained

1 can (12 ounces) evaporated milk

Paprika for sprinkling

In a large saucepan over medium heat, cook the onion and garlic in the butter until tender and transparent, 5 to 7 minutes. Add the potatoes, bell pepper, broth, black pepper, marjoram, bay leaves, and nutmeg. Bring to a boil, then reduce heat to low, and simmer for about 20 minutes, or until the potatoes are tender, stirring occasionally. Stir in the remaining ingredients, except the paprika. Bring to a boil again, then reduce heat to low and simmer for 1 to 2 minutes, stirring frequently. **Remove the bay leaves** and serve, sprinkling each serving lightly with paprika.

Soups and Chowders

Cream of Broccoli and Cheddar Soup

4 cups

Did ya' ever think that maybe the settlers of the Old West really
headed out that way for the vegetables and not the gold?
Well, broccoli sure is "good as gold" this way!
(And it's as easy as using the blender!)

1   pound fresh broccoli (about 1 medium-sized head)
14 ounces chicken broth
2   tablespoons butter
2   tablespoons all-purpose flour

2   cups milk
¼   teaspoon freshly ground black pepper
2   cups (8 ounces) shredded Cheddar cheese

Clean the broccoli, then chop the florets and thinly slice the stems. In a medium-sized saucepan, combine the broccoli and chicken broth; heat to a boil. Reduce heat and simmer, covered, for about 7 minutes or until the broccoli is fork-tender. Transfer, one third at a time, to a food processor or blender. Process until fairly smooth. In the same saucepan, melt the butter over medium heat; add the flour. Cook, stirring constantly, until bubbly. Add the milk and pepper; heat to a boil, stirring constantly. Reduce heat to medium and add the broccoli purée. Stir in the cheese; heat just until the cheese melts (do not boil), stirring constantly.

NOTE: For a chunky broccoli and Cheddar soup, reserve 1 cup of the broccoli pieces and add them to the soup with the broccoli purée.

Italian Lentil Stew

about 4 servings

There's nothing like a thick, rich, stewlike soup to satisfy even the biggest appetites. And did you know that our Western states grow lentils so we can have lots of thick, rich goodness for all of our popular Italian-style dishes?!

1 cup lentils, rinsed	1 cup chopped onion
14½ ounces beef broth (from a can or granules)	2 garlic cloves, minced
1 bay leaf	1 can (14½ ounces) Italian-style stewed tomatoes
8 ounces bulk Italian sausage	

In a medium-sized saucepan, combine the lentils, beef broth, and bay leaf. Bring to a boil, then reduce heat and simmer, covered, until the lentils are just tender, about 15 minutes. Meanwhile, in a large skillet, cook the sausage over medium-high heat until browned, stirring to break up into small pieces. Add the onion and garlic and cook until just tender, about 5 minutes. Spoon off any excess fat, then stir in the lentil mixture and the stewed tomatoes. Bring to a boil. **Remove the bay leaf before serving.**

NOTE: If you use Italian link sausage, squeeze the sausage out of the casing so it can be broken up into small pieces as it browns.

Manhattan Clam Chowder

about 9 cups

"I'll take Manhattan" . . . clam chowder, that is!
You'll taste why.

¼ cup chopped onion
1 celery stalk, chopped
1 carrot, chopped
2 tablespoons butter
3 cans (6½ ounces each) chopped clams
1 can (10½ ounces) chicken broth
1 bottle (8 ounces) clam juice
1 cup diced potatoes, uncooked (1 small- to medium-sized potato)
1 can (28 ounces) whole tomatoes, cut up
½ teaspoon salt
¼ teaspoon pepper
¼ teaspoon dried thyme
1 bay leaf

In a soup pot over medium heat, cook the onion, celery, and carrot in the butter for 3 to 5 minutes, or until tender. Add the remaining ingredients and bring to a boil, stirring occasionally. Reduce heat to low and simmer for 8 to 10 minutes, or until the potatoes are tender. **Remove the bay leaf before serving.**

New England Clam Chowder

about 7 cups

New Englanders are **very** *proud of their "chowda," and you'll be proud, too, when you serve this easy version tonight.*

¼ cup chopped onion

2 tablespoons butter

2 cans (6½ ounces each) chopped clams

1 bottle (8 ounces) clam juice

1 can (10½ ounces) chicken broth

1 cup diced potatoes

¼ teaspoon salt

¼ teaspoon pepper

1 teaspoon dried parsley flakes

⅓ cup cornstarch

3 cups milk

In a soup pot over medium heat, sauté the onions in the butter for 3 to 5 minutes, or until tender. Add the clams, clam juice, chicken broth, potatoes, salt, pepper, and parsley; cook for 15 minutes or until the potatoes are tender. In a small bowl, dissolve the cornstarch in the milk. Add to the soup pot, then bring to a boil. Cook until thickened, 5 to 8 minutes, stirring constantly.

Parsnip and Spinach Cream Soup

about 9 cups

There's nothing like a full-flavored soup, and this one delivers
surprise goodness for our bodies as well as our taste buds.
Well, look how strong Popeye is—that's why the kids'll
love it, too. Oh!! No parsnips? Use carrots instead.
(Parsnips might be a bit sweeter, though.)

1½ pounds fresh parsnips, peeled and cut into ¼-inch slices	5 ounces (½ of a 10-ounce bag) fresh spinach
1 medium-sized onion, thinly sliced	¼ cup Dijon-style mustard
1 celery stalk, thinly sliced	1½ cups heavy cream or half-and-half
1½ quarts chicken broth	½ teaspoon pepper, or to taste

In a soup pot, cook the parsnips, onion, and celery in the chicken broth. Bring to a boil, then reduce heat to medium and cook for 20 to 30 minutes, or until tender. Remove from heat and stir in the spinach. Place the mixture in a blender or food processor and purée until smooth; return the mixture to the pot. Stir in the remaining ingredients. Serve hot or chilled.

Pasta Gumbo

8 to 10 servings

Looking for a satisfying one-pot meal?
You've found it!

2 garlic cloves, crushed
1 cup chopped onion
¼ cup (½ stick) butter
1 can (28 ounces) whole tomatoes, broken up, undrained
4 cups water
2 bottles (8 ounces each) clam juice
1 teaspoon salt
1 teaspoon dried oregano
2 bay leaves
¼ teaspoon hot pepper sauce

½ teaspoon garlic powder
⅛ teaspoon cayenne pepper
1 teaspoon Cajun seasoning
8 ounces ditalini (or other small pasta shape)
1 can (14¼ ounces) okra, drained, or 1 frozen package (10 ounces), thawed
1 package (8 ounces) imitation crabmeat, broken up
2 cans (4¼ ounces each) baby shrimp, drained
1 can (8 ounces) boned crabmeat, drained

In a large pot over medium-high heat, sauté the garlic and onion in the butter until golden, about 5 minutes. Add the tomatoes, water, clam juice, salt, oregano, bay leaves, hot pepper sauce, garlic powder, cayenne pepper, and Cajun seasoning. Reduce heat to low and simmer, covered, for 40 minutes. Bring to a boil, gradually add the pasta, reduce the heat to medium, and cook, covered, for about 15 minutes, or until the pasta is tender, stirring occasionally. Stir in the remaining ingredients and cook for 5 minutes more. **Remove the bay leaves before serving.**

NOTE: For more of a "kick," double the Cajun seasoning.

Perfect Split Pea Soup

about 6 cups

Perfectly thick, perfectly rich . . . just the way they make it in the Mountain West.

1 cup green split peas (from a 1-pound package)	½ teaspoon pepper
½ cup barley	¾ pound diced ham or smoked turkey
1 small onion, diced	8 cups water, divided
½ of a carrot, shredded	½ teaspoon baking soda
½ teaspoon garlic salt	

In a soup pot, combine the split peas, barley, onion, carrot, garlic salt, pepper, ham, and 5 cups of the water. Boil over medium heat for 1½ hours, adding 1 cup of water every 20 minutes for the first hour of cooking, stirring occasionally. Add the baking soda. Stir until the soup thickens, 8 to 10 minutes.

Seafood Chowder

8 to 12 servings (about 2 quarts)

*On a blustery day in Boston, this is how they
whip up a chowder that warms to the bones!*

1 large onion, chopped
3 celery stalks, sliced
3 potatoes, peeled and chopped
3 tablespoons butter
1 can (8 ounces) tomato sauce
1 can (14½ ounces) whole tomatoes
1 can (10½ ounces) chicken broth

1 bay leaf
1 teaspoon dried basil
1 teaspoon garlic powder
1 teaspoon dried oregano
½ teaspoon salt
¼ teaspoon pepper
2 pounds cod, haddock, or sole fillets, cut into 1-inch cubes

In a soup pot over low heat, sauté the onion, celery, and potatoes in the butter until the onion is softened. Add the remaining ingredients, except the fish. Cover and simmer for 20 minutes. Add the fish and simmer for 15 minutes more. **Be sure to remove the bay leaf before serving.**

NOTE: If you'd like, try using 1 pound of fish and adding, at the same time, one 6½-ounce can of chopped clams and 1 pound of peeled, deveined, and chopped shrimp.

Chicken and Turkey

All-American Oven-"Fried" Drumsticks

4 servings

*Years ago the only fried chicken was Southern-fried, and there's
no doubt that it's delicious, but oven-"fried" has its merits, too.
This way, we can have the best of everything.*

¼ cup all-purpose flour
2 eggs
¼ cup milk
1 cup fine dry bread crumbs
¼ teaspoon dried oregano
¼ teaspoon garlic powder
¼ teaspoon onion powder

½ teaspoon salt
¼ teaspoon pepper
½ teaspoon paprika
¼ teaspoon dried basil
8 chicken drumsticks
3 tablespoons butter

Preheat the oven to 350°F. Place the flour in a shallow dish. In
a second shallow dish, beat the eggs with the milk, just until mixed.
In a plastic bag, mix together the bread crumbs and seasonings.
Dredge the chicken in the flour, one or two pieces at a time, coating
both sides evenly. Dip the floured chicken pieces into the egg mixture, then place in the bread crumb mixture; close the bag and shake
to coat well. Place the butter in a large baking dish and melt in the
oven. Arrange the chicken in a single layer over the melted butter,
turning to coat both sides. Bake for 25 minutes; turn the chicken
and bake for an additional 25 minutes, or until golden brown and
no pink remains.

Baja Chicken

3 to 4 servings

Looking for an easy way to spice up your life? Here's how!
Do it like they do in Baja.

1 tablespoon vegetable oil	2 tablespoons chopped fresh parsley
½ cup chopped onion (about ½ of a small onion)	¼ cup water
1 garlic clove, crushed	1½ pounds ripe tomatoes, (about 2 large), cut into ¼-inch cubes
1½ teaspoons chili powder	
¼ teaspoon ground cumin	2 chicken breasts, split, skinned, and boned (about 1 pound)
¾ teaspoon salt	
¼ teaspoon pepper	

In a large skillet, heat the oil over medium-high heat; add the onion and garlic and sauté until the onion is transparent, about 5 minutes. Add the chili powder, cumin, salt, pepper, parsley, water, and tomatoes; reduce heat to low, cover, and simmer for 5 minutes, stirring occasionally. Add the chicken breasts, cover, and simmer for about 15 minutes, or until a fork can be inserted into the chicken with ease and no pink remains, occasionally spooning the sauce over the chicken.

NOTE: Serve over hot cooked rice or pasta.

California Fiesta Chicken and Rice

about 6 servings

*You'll feel like celebrating when you taste this. It'll have
everybody saying, "OOH it's so BUENO!!™"*

1 tablespoon vegetable oil	1 can (17 ounces) whole-kernel corn, drained
2 pounds chicken breasts, skinned, boned, and cut into 1-inch cubes	1 package (about 1.25 ounces) chili seasoning mix
1 can (14½ ounces) chicken broth	1 can (4 ounces) chopped green chilies, drained
1 can (15 ounces) tomato sauce	2 cups instant rice, uncooked

In a large skillet, heat the oil over medium-high heat; add the chicken and brown for 3 to 5 minutes or until light golden. Add the broth, tomato sauce, corn, chili seasoning, and green chilies. Bring to a boil, stirring occasionally; reduce heat, cover, and simmer for 5 minutes. Stir in the rice and remove from the heat. Cover and let stand for about 7 minutes, or until the rice is done.

Chili'd Chicken

4 servings

*Why didn't we think of this before?! Why, it's a whole meal.
(I think the folks in Texas have been keeping it a secret!)*

2 tablespoons vegetable oil, divided
1 medium-sized onion, chopped
3 tablespoons chili powder
2 cans (15 ounces each) kidney beans, rinsed and drained
8 chicken thighs, skinned
1 can (28 ounces) whole tomatoes, drained (juice reserved), and chopped
¼ cup shredded Cheddar cheese

Preheat the oven to 350°F. In a small skillet, heat 1 tablespoon of the oil over medium heat. Add the chopped onion and cook for 3 to 5 minutes or until soft; set aside. In a medium-sized bowl, mix together the onions, chili powder, and kidney beans; set aside. Lightly oil a 9" × 13" baking pan with the remaining oil; add the kidney bean mixture. Arrange the chicken over the top of the beans, pressing the chicken into the bean mixture. Spoon the tomatoes over the beans and chicken and add the reserved tomato juice. Bake for about 65 minutes. Remove from the oven, sprinkle with the shredded cheese, and bake for 10 minutes more or until the cheese is melted and the chicken is fork tender and no pink remains.

Chinatown Chicken Tenders

2 to 3 servings

*There's nothing like the flavor combination of spicy hot
and sweet tangy flavors that we get in Chinese food.
Here's how we can get those tastes at home!*

2 tablespoons vegetable oil

1 pound chicken breasts, skinned, boned, and cut into finger-sized pieces

1 tablespoon cornstarch

SAUCE

1½ cups chicken broth

2 tablespoons tomato or spaghetti sauce

1 tablespoon soy sauce

1 tablespoon honey

½ teaspoon ground ginger

4 garlic cloves, minced

½ teaspoon hot pepper sauce

In a large skillet, heat the oil over medium heat; add the chicken pieces and sauté until golden, 5 to 7 minutes. Meanwhile, in a medium-sized bowl, combine the sauce ingredients; set aside ¼ cup of the sauce mixture. Pour the remaining sauce over the chicken. Reduce heat to medium-low, cover partially, and simmer for 5 minutes. Add the cornstarch to the reserved ¼ cup of sauce and blend; pour over the chicken and continue cooking, uncovered, for 5 to 7 minutes, or until the sauce starts to thicken, stirring occasionally.

NOTE: Serve over 2 cups of hot cooked rice.

Fettuccine with Chicken and Lobster Sauce

4 servings

*A classic dish that uses a few shortcuts and is ready
in minutes. (But it'll take your gang ages
to stop raving about it!)*

1   garlic clove, minced

½   of a medium-sized onion,
    chopped (about 1 cup)

1   tablespoon butter

1   can (10½ ounces) condensed
    lobster bisque

1   cup milk

¼   cup grated Parmesan cheese,
    plus extra for topping

1½ cups cooked skinless,
    boneless chicken breasts,
    cut into strips (about 1½
    chicken breasts)

3   cups hot cooked fettuccine
    (about ½ of a 16-ounce
    package)

Freshly ground black pepper
(optional)

In a large skillet over medium heat, sauté the garlic and onion
in the butter for 3 to 5 minutes, stirring constantly. Stir in the bisque,
milk, and ¼ cup cheese. Bring to a boil; add the chicken. Reduce
heat to low and cook for 5 minutes, stirring often. Add the fettuccine.
Sprinkle with grated Parmesan cheese and freshly ground pepper,
if desired. Serve immediately.

Finger Lakes Company Chicken

4 servings

Did you know that some great wines come from the Finger Lakes region of New York State? Well, they do—and here's a recipe that gives us a way to include a bit of it in our cooking, while letting our company know how special they are! (And it's, well, what you'd call an anybody-can-do-it "snap"!)

½ cup seasoned bread crumbs	4 thin slices Muenster cheese
2 chicken breasts, split, skinned, boned, and flattened (about 1 pound)	¼ cup dry white wine

Preheat the oven to 350°F. Place the bread crumbs in a shallow dish and dredge the chicken, coating well. Place the chicken in an 8-inch-square baking dish that has been coated with nonstick vegetable spray. Bake for 15 minutes. Remove the chicken from the oven and top each piece with a cheese slice; pour the wine evenly over the top. Bake for an additional 15 minutes or until the chicken is done and no pink remains, and the cheese is bubbly and light brown.

Frontier Chicken and Noodle Casserole

5 to 6 servings

I don't know if Davy Crockett had meals like this, but I'm sure he'd have loved it—and so will your family. It's robust and delicious, and the simplest dish you could imagine.

1	pound cooked, boneless chicken breasts, cubed	2	cups cooked fine egg noodles
3	celery stalks, chopped	¼	cup mayonnaise
1	teaspoon onion powder	1	can (10¾ ounces) cream of chicken soup
¼	teaspoon salt	1	cup crushed potato chips (1 6-ounce bag equals about 2 cups crushed)
¼	teaspoon pepper		

Preheat the oven to 350°F. In a large bowl, combine all the ingredients except the potato chips; mix well. Spoon the mixture into a 2-quart casserole dish that has been coated with nonstick vegetable spray. Top with the crushed chips. Bake for 30 minutes or until golden.

Garden Skillet Chicken

4 servings

Here's an easy, mouth-watering way to enjoy the bounty of our backyard garden. (And since it's made all in one pan, that sure helps with the "easy" part!)

2 tablespoons vegetable oil, divided

2 chicken breasts, split, skinned, boned, and cut into 1-inch pieces

2 small zucchini, cut into ¼-inch slices

1 small yellow squash, cut into ¼-inch slices

1 medium-sized onion, cut into eighths

1 medium-sized red bell pepper, cut into 1-inch strips

3 garlic cloves, minced

½ cup chicken broth

¼ cup dry white wine

1¼ teaspoons salt

½ teaspoon black pepper

1½ teaspoons dried basil

1½ teaspoons dried oregano

2 medium-sized tomatoes, cut into chunks

8 ounces (½ of a 1-pound package) linguine, cooked

¾ cup grated Parmesan cheese

In a large skillet, heat 1 tablespoon of the oil over medium-high heat; add the chicken and cook, stirring occasionally, for about 5 minutes or until the chicken is browned and fork tender. Remove the chicken from the skillet and set aside. In the same skillet, add the remaining 1 tablespoon oil and heat; add the zucchini, yellow squash, onion, red pepper, and garlic. Cook for 5 minutes, stirring occasionally. Add the chicken and mix well; add the broth, wine, salt, black pepper, basil, and oregano and cook for 3 minutes more. Add the tomatoes and heat through. Toss with the hot cooked linguine and the Parmesan cheese, and serve.

NOTE: This is so hearty and tasty, you could make it without the chicken breast and no one would miss it!

Herbed Chicken and Mushrooms

3 to 4 servings

When you need something to serve to company or maybe that special friend, check out this tasty combination of herbs for a touch of class that's a sure winner!

1 pound chicken breasts, skinned and boned	¼ cup dry white wine
1 tablespoon all-purpose flour	¼ cup chicken broth
⅛ teaspoon salt	¼ teaspoon dried rosemary
Pinch of pepper	¼ teaspoon dried thyme
1 tablespoon vegetable oil	¼ teaspoon ground tarragon
1 tablespoon butter	¼ teaspoon ground marjoram
½ pound fresh mushrooms, sliced	½ teaspoon garlic powder

Pound the chicken to ½-inch thickness. In a shallow dish, combine the flour, salt, and pepper. Lightly coat the chicken with the flour mixture. In a large skillet, heat the oil and butter over medium-high heat; add the chicken and cook for 3 to 4 minutes on each side, or until tender and no pink remains. Remove the chicken; keep warm. In the same skillet, add the remaining ingredients and cook for 3 to 4 minutes; pour over the chicken and serve.

Honeyed Chicken Breasts

4 to 6 servings
(1 cup sauce)

Americans love to barbecue **and** *we love chicken. Here's a "honey" of a way to combine both passions, with down-home-tasting, quick-cooking chicken breasts.*

6 to 8 chicken breast halves, (*not* skinless and boneless)
¼ cup honey
¼ cup vegetable oil
¼ cup mayonnaise
2 tablespoons prepared mustard

1 tablespoon white vinegar
1 tablespoon Worcestershire sauce
½ teaspoon onion powder

Preheat a barbecue grill. Place the chicken breast halves on the grill and cook for 20 to 30 minutes or until no pink remains. Meanwhile, in a medium-sized bowl, combine the remaining ingredients, then brush over the cooked chicken. Grill the chicken for 5 minutes more.

NOTE: You might want to give this a little more snap by adding some chopped scallions to the honey glaze.

Key West Grilled Chicken

4 to 6 servings

It seems like it's always party time in Key West—now you can bring home some of the festivities!

1½ pounds chicken breasts, split, skinned, and boned
3 tablespoons soy sauce
1 teaspoon lime juice
1 teaspoon garlic powder
1 tablespoon honey
1 tablespoon vegetable oil

Place the chicken in a shallow dish; set aside. In a small bowl, mix together the remaining ingredients; pour the mixture over the chicken. Cover and marinate in the refrigerator for 1 hour, turning occasionally. Preheat a barbecue grill. Cook the chicken on medium heat for about 10 minutes on each side, or until tender and no pink remains. Discard excess marinade.

NOTE: This works great in your broiler, too.

Lemon Pepper Chicken

6 servings

This combination may have a strong tie to trendy California, but North, South, East, West—seems we all like chicken best, especially when it's this easy!

1 cup Italian dressing	2¼ teaspoons pepper
⅔ cup powdered lemonade-flavor drink mix	3 whole chicken breasts, split, skinned, and boned

In a medium-sized bowl, mix together the dressing, lemonade mix, and pepper. Stir well and add the chicken. Cover and marinate the chicken in the refrigerator for about 8 hours, or overnight. Preheat the broiler. Place the chicken on the broiler pan, discarding the marinade. Broil the chicken for 3 to 5 minutes on each side, or until a fork can be inserted into the chicken with ease and no pink remains.

NOTE: This works great on your barbecue grill, too!

Lime-Baked Walnut Chicken

4 servings

Lots of Floridians have lime trees right in their own yards.
(I have three of them!) This dish can make you feel
like you do, too!

½ cup all-purpose flour
½ cup finely chopped walnuts
1 teaspoon paprika
¾ teaspoon salt
⅛ teaspoon pepper
¾ teaspoon grated lime peel

½ teaspoon garlic powder
½ cup lime juice
1 2½- to 3-pound chicken, cut into 8 pieces
¼ cup vegetable oil

Preheat the oven to 350°F. Line a cookie sheet with foil and coat with nonstick vegetable spray; set aside. In a shallow dish, combine the flour, walnuts, paprika, salt, pepper, lime peel, and garlic powder. Place the lime juice in another shallow dish. Dip the chicken pieces in the juice, then coat with the walnut mixture, pressing it onto the chicken with the back of a spoon. Place the coated chicken in a single layer on the prepared cookie sheet; drizzle the oil over the top. Bake for 50 to 60 minutes or until the chicken is golden and no pink remains.

Louisiana Chicken

6 to 8 servings

Let's face it—there's so much good food in Louisiana that it's like the world's taste headquarters. This is a family-type dish that proves the point. Why, it's so full-flavored that it's bound to become a classic at your house. (It already is at mine!)

¼ to ½ cup vegetable oil	3 medium-sized green bell peppers, cut into thin strips
2 chickens (2½ to 3 pounds each), each cut into 8 pieces	2 medium-sized onions, diced
½ cup all-purpose flour	3 cups chicken broth
4 medium-sized celery stalks, thinly sliced	2¼ teaspoons salt
	½ teaspoon hot pepper sauce

Preheat the oven to 350°F. In a large skillet, heat ¼ cup oil over medium-high heat; cook the chicken, a few pieces at a time, until browned on all sides, adding additional oil as needed. Remove the browned chicken to two 9" × 13" baking pans that have been coated with nonstick vegetable spray, dividing the pieces evenly between the 2 pans; set aside. Add the flour to the skillet juices and cook over medium heat for about 30 seconds or until the flour is golden, stirring constantly. Add the celery, green peppers, and onions; cook for about 5 minutes, or until the vegetables are tender, stirring frequently. Stir in the remaining ingredients. Bring the mixture to a boil, then pour over the chicken, dividing it evenly between the 2 pans. Bake, uncovered, for 50 to 60 minutes, or until the chicken is fork-tender and no pink remains, basting occasionally.

NOTE: You can easily cut this recipe in half, but for the same work, why not make it all and freeze the leftovers for a later date—it'll taste just as good!! Serve over hot cooked rice.

North End Skillet Chicken

about 3 servings

*Just imagine how different our history might be if Paul Revere had
stayed home that eventful night . . . and he just might have,
if Mrs. Revere had served this!! (Then again, she
wouldn't have been able to take these shortcuts,
'cause I doubt she had onion soup mix in
her cupboard!)*

1   envelope (from a 2-ounce box) onion or onion-mushroom soup mix

¼   cup vegetable or olive oil

¼   cup water

1   tablespoon fresh lime or lemon juice

⅛   teaspoon cayenne pepper

1   teaspoon Italian seasoning

½   teaspoon garlic powder

1   pound chicken breasts, skinned, boned, and cut into thin strips

1   package (16 ounces) frozen assorted vegetables, thawed and drained

In a large skillet, blend the onion soup mix, oil, water, lime juice, red pepper, Italian seasoning, and garlic powder; let stand for 5 minutes. Bring the mixture to a boil and stir in the chicken and vegetables. Cook, uncovered, for 8 to 10 minutes, or until chicken is done and no pink remains, stirring frequently.

NOTE: Serve over hot cooked rice.

North/South Chicken

4 servings

This one teams our Southern pecans with our
*Northern cranberries, so we **all** win!*

2   chicken breasts, split,
    skinned, and boned
½   cup pecan pieces, finely
    chopped
⅓   cup seasoned bread crumbs
1   teaspoon grated orange peel

¼   teaspoon salt
¼   teaspoon paprika
¼   cup honey
1   tablespoon orange juice
1   can (16 ounces) whole berry
    cranberry sauce

Preheat the oven to 350°F. Place the chicken in a shallow dish. In another shallow dish, mix together the pecans, bread crumbs, orange peel, salt, and paprika. In a small bowl, combine the honey and orange juice. Lightly spread the honey mixture over the chicken pieces; place the chicken in the crumb mixture, turning to coat on all sides. Arrange the chicken in a 9" × 13" baking dish that has been coated with nonstick vegetable spray. Bake for 35 to 45 minutes or until the chicken is fork tender and no pink remains. Top each serving with a small amount of cranberry sauce; serve with the remaining cranberry sauce.

Santa Fe Chicken Tostados

6 servings

I bet you'll hear shouts of "Olé!"
when you treat them to this!

6 6-inch corn tortillas
2 teaspoons vegetable oil
1 pound chicken breasts, skinned, boned, and cut into thin strips
2 scallions, sliced

1 package (1.25 ounces) taco seasoning mix
½ cup water
1 can (15 ounces) black beans, well drained
¾ cup shredded Cheddar cheese

Preheat the oven to 375°F. Place the tortillas flat on an ungreased baking sheet and bake for 5 to 7 minutes, or until crisp; set aside. Meanwhile, in a large skillet, heat the oil over medium-high heat; add the chicken and sauté for 3 minutes. Add the scallions, taco seasoning mix, and water. Reduce the heat and simmer for 5 minutes. Add the black beans and simmer for 2 minutes more; remove from heat. Spoon ½ cup of the chicken mixture onto each tortilla; top each with 2 teaspoons Cheddar cheese and bake for 2 to 3 minutes, or until the cheese melts.

NOTE: For an authentic Southwestern touch, garnish with chopped tomatoes and sour cream.

South-of-the-Border Chicken Chili

6 to 8 servings

*Two all-time favorites, chicken and chili, combined in one dish
that you will love making and your family will love eating.*

1 can (16 ounces) refried beans
1 can (16 ounces) baked beans
1 jar (16 ounces) chunky-style salsa
¼ cup ketchup

2 chicken breasts, split, skinned, boned, and cut into 1-inch chunks
½ cup shredded Monterey Jack cheese

Preheat the oven to 350°F. In a 2½-quart casserole dish, combine the refried beans, baked beans, salsa, ketchup, and chicken. Cover and bake for 1 hour, stirring occasionally, until the chicken is tender and no pink remains. Remove from the oven and sprinkle with the shredded cheese; cover and bake for 5 minutes more or until the cheese is melted.

NOTE: Serve in bowls, maybe with some crusty bread. Mmm!

South Philly Chicken Parmesan

4 to 6 servings

*Stay home and enjoy the tastes of Italy. Why, after they
taste this, your kitchen will have a new name:
"Little Italy"!*

⅓ cup seasoned bread crumbs

3 chicken breasts, split,
skinned, and boned

2 tablespoons olive oil, plus
more as needed

1 jar (14 ounces) prepared
spaghetti sauce (about 1½
cups)

2 cups (8 ounces) shredded
mozzarella cheese

2 tablespoons Parmesan cheese

Preheat the oven to 350°F. Place the bread crumbs in a shallow
dish. Coat the chicken evenly on both sides with the bread crumbs.
In a large skillet, heat the oil over medium-high heat. Place the
chicken in the skillet, 3 pieces at a time, and cook for 2 to 3 minutes
per side, or until golden, adding more oil if needed. Pour half of the
spaghetti sauce evenly into a 9" × 13" baking dish. Place the chicken
in the baking dish and pour the remaining sauce over the chicken.
Sprinkle with the mozzarella cheese, then the Parmesan cheese.
Bake for 35 to 40 minutes, or until a fork can be inserted into the
chicken with ease and no pink remains.

Special Chicken Salad

about 4 servings (4 cups)

When I first saw this recipe in Palm Springs, California, I said, "Oh, no!!" I didn't think I'd like the combination, but then I tried it and, WOW!! It's that special! But you don't need a special occasion to serve this, 'cause it'll make your family feel special. (And it's so easy!)

1 cup mayonnaise	3 cups cubed, cooked chicken
1 tablespoon honey	1 cup seedless grapes
½ teaspoon curry powder	½ cup pecan halves
¼ teaspoon celery salt	

In a large bowl, mix together the mayonnaise, honey, curry powder, and celery salt. Mix in the chicken, grapes, and pecans. Cover and refrigerate until ready to serve.

NOTE: You can use cooked turkey instead of chicken, if you'd like.

Summer Turkey Supper

4 to 5 servings

*The Caribbean tastes have caught on everywhere, and here's
a way to capture those wonderful flavors with an easy
"throw-together" that'll make you look
like a kitchen whiz.*

3 cups cooked rice

1 teaspoon curry powder

2 cups diced roast turkey

2 tablespoons finely chopped onion

6 to 8 pimiento-stuffed green olives, sliced

1 can (10½ ounces) condensed cream of mushroom soup

½ cup milk

½ cup shredded Cheddar cheese

Preheat the oven to 350°F. In a medium-sized bowl, combine the rice and curry powder. Place the rice evenly over the bottom of a greased 9-inch-square baking pan. Cover with the turkey, onion, and olives. In a small bowl, combine the soup and milk; pour over the turkey mixture. Top with the cheese, then bake for about 30 minutes or until the cheese melts.

NOTE: Use leftover turkey, or one of the many brands of precooked turkey that are available in the market—do whatever is easiest!

Turkey Burritos

4 servings

There's more than one way to fill a tortilla, amigo—
just try this and you'll see.

8   ounces cooked boneless turkey breast, shredded (about 1½ cups)
½   cup salsa, divided
1   can (16 ounces) refried beans
¼   teaspoon salt
1   teaspoon ground cumin
½   teaspoon chili powder

8   7-inch flour tortillas
½   cup chopped tomatoes (about ½ of a large tomato)
¾   cup (3 ounces) shredded Cheddar or Monterey Jack cheese
Guacamole for topping (optional)
Sour cream for topping (optional)

Place the turkey in a shallow bowl and cover with ⅓ cup of the salsa. Cover and marinate in the refrigerator for 1 hour. Preheat the oven to 350°F. In a small saucepan, heat the beans, the remaining salsa, salt, cumin, and chili powder over medium heat, stirring constantly. Spoon about 2 tablespoons of the bean mixture down the center of each tortilla; top with equal amounts of the marinated turkey, then the tomatoes, then the cheese. (Discard excess marinade.) Fold one edge of each tortilla over the filling; fold in the sides and roll. Place the prepared tortillas on a baking sheet, seam side down, and bake for 10 minutes, or until the cheese is melted. Before serving, top each burrito with a dollop of guacamole and sour cream, if desired.

Turkey "Crab" Cakes

8 patties

*For that "Gee, what do I feel like having?" night—
never again will we have to wonder what to
do with that little bit of leftover turkey.*

2 cups shredded cooked white or dark turkey
1 cup seasoned bread crumbs
1 small onion, finely chopped
1 teaspoon salt
4 tablespoons mayonnaise
1 teaspoon prepared mustard
1 teaspoon Worcestershire sauce
½ teaspoon prepared horseradish
2 eggs, beaten
1 teaspoon seafood seasoning
¼ cup vegetable oil

In a medium-sized bowl, mix together the turkey, bread crumbs, onion, and salt. In another medium-sized bowl, combine the remaining ingredients, except the oil. Add the mayonnaise mixture to the turkey mixture and mix well. Form the mixture into patties. In a large skillet, heat the oil over medium-high heat. Add the patties and cook for about 5 minutes on each side, until brown and done.

NOTE: There are many brands of precooked turkey available in the market, so you don't even have to start cooking a whole turkey to enjoy these!

Turkey Strata

6 servings

North Carolina cooks tell me this is a favorite.
Why not give it a whirl?

2	cups seasoned croutons	1	cup milk
1½	cups (about 6 ounces) turkey ham, cut into ¼-inch cubes	4	eggs, beaten
		2	teaspoons prepared mustard
1	cup (4 ounces) shredded Cheddar cheese	¼	teaspoon white pepper

Layer the croutons, then the turkey ham, then the cheese in an 8-inch-square glass baking dish that has been coated with nonstick vegetable spray. In a small bowl, combine the remaining ingredients; mix well. Pour over the cheese layer. Cover and refrigerate overnight. Uncover the baking dish and place it in a cold oven. Set the oven temperature to 350°F. and bake the strata for 35 to 40 minutes, or until a knife inserted in the center comes out clean. Let stand for 5 minutes before slicing.

NOTE: This works just as well when the turkey ham is lightly chopped in a food processor.

Western Turkey Quiche

6 to 8 servings

*C'mon, real men **do** eat quiche (especially when it's made like this)! Just ask the cowboys!*

⅔ cup diced turkey ham
½ cup shredded Cheddar cheese
1 unbaked 9-inch pie shell

3 eggs, beaten
¾ cup milk

Preheat the oven to 350°F. In a large bowl, combine the turkey ham and the cheese; spread evenly in the pie shell. In a small bowl, whisk together the eggs and milk; pour evenly into the pie shell. Place the filled pie shell on a cookie sheet and bake for 45 to 55 minutes, or until a knife inserted in the center comes out clean.

American-Style Hot Veal Sausage

16 patties
(4 to 5 servings)

The one-of-a-kind smell and taste of a blue-ribbon winner
at the county fair! I love it with
fried peppers and onions.

2 pounds ground veal
1 teaspoon whole fennel seed
1 teaspoon crushed red pepper
1 teaspoon salt
1 teaspoon black pepper

1 teaspoon garlic powder
½ teaspoon paprika
1 teaspoon dried thyme leaves
½ teaspoon onion powder
4 teaspoons vegetable oil, divided

In a large bowl, combine all the ingredients except the oil; mix thoroughly. Shape the mixture into 16 patties. Coat the bottom of a large skillet with 2 teaspoons of the oil and add just enough water (about ¼ cup) to cover the bottom; heat over medium heat. Add half the patties, making sure they don't touch; cook thoroughly, uncovered, for about 5 minutes on each side, or until brown. Repeat, using the additional 2 teaspoons oil and more water.

Beef Stew Weekend

about 4 servings

In the Midwest, it's almost a rule to serve this regularly ('cause nothing warms us better at the end of a long, cold day). Great for doubling, too—then when it's rewarmed, it's even better.

1½ pounds lean beef chuck, cut into 1-inch cubes

2 teaspoons olive or vegetable oil

1 large onion, cut into thin wedges

2 garlic cloves, minced

1 can (28 ounces) plum tomatoes, undrained, coarsely chopped

1 large baking potato, peeled and cut into ¾-inch chunks

⅔ cup mild picante sauce

1 teaspoon dried basil

½ teaspoon dried oregano

½ teaspoon salt (optional)

1 large green bell pepper, coarsely chopped

1 large zucchini, sliced into ½-inch-thick rounds

¼ cup grated Parmesan cheese

Preheat the broiler. Place the meat on the rack of a broiler pan and broil 4 inches from the heat until lightly browned, turning once. Meanwhile, in a large saucepan, heat the oil over medium heat. Add the onion and garlic and cook for 3 minutes. Add the browned meat, tomatoes, potato, picante sauce, basil, oregano, and salt. Bring to a boil, then reduce heat to low. Cover and simmer until the meat is tender, about 1 hour. Stir in the green pepper and zucchini. Continue to simmer until the vegetables are crisp-tender, about 10 to 15 minutes more. Ladle into bowls, sprinkle with Parmesan cheese, and serve.

NOTE: Serve with additional picante sauce, if desired.

Better-Than-Ever Meat Loaf

6 to 8 servings

*Meat loaf is an American favorite, along with Mom and apple pie.
I know that most everybody has a favorite way they like
meat loaf, but this one's sure worth a try. It even got a
load of votes in the meat loaf competition.*

2	pounds ground beef	⅔	cup ketchup, divided
1½	cups fresh bread crumbs	½	teaspoon salt
2	eggs	½	teaspoon pepper
¾	cup water	½	teaspoon garlic powder

Preheat the oven to 350°F. In a large bowl, combine all the ingredients except ⅓ cup ketchup; mix well. Place the mixture in a large baking pan that has been coated with nonstick vegetable spray and shape into a loaf. Spread the remaining ⅓ cup ketchup over the top. Bake for 1 hour or until done.

NOTE: Very lean ground turkey or chicken works great, too. If you want to cook this in the microwave, simply combine the ingredients as above, then place the mixture in a 2-quart oblong microwaveable baking dish and shape into a loaf. Microwave, uncovered, on High (full power), turning the dish occasionally, for 25 minutes or until done. Remove from the baking dish and let stand, covered, for 5 minutes before serving.

Black-eyed Pea Skillet

about 4 servings

Southern cooks have always known how good this one-pot meal is for us—'cause they've been serving it for years.

1 pound ground beef	1 can (14½ ounces) whole tomatoes, undrained and coarsely chopped
1½ cups chopped onion	
1 cup chopped green bell pepper	½ teaspoon salt
2 cans (16 ounces each) black-eyed peas, drained	¼ teaspoon black pepper

In a large skillet, cook the ground beef, onion, and green pepper over medium heat until the beef is browned, stirring to crumble the meat; drain off the liquid. Add the remaining ingredients; bring to a boil, reduce heat, and simmer for 30 minutes, stirring often.

NOTE: Go ahead and add your own seasoning favorites. Anything from basil to oregano, chili powder, hot pepper sauce, or Cajun seasoning will work.

Broiled Steak with Spicy Potatoes

4 servings

(⅓ cup Spicy Seasoning Mix)

In the Midwest, a hearty, satisfying meal is the rule.
And, boy, does this one satisfy!

SPICY SEASONING MIX

3	tablespoons chili powder
2	teaspoons ground coriander
2	teaspoons ground cumin
1½	teaspoons garlic powder
1	teaspoon dried oregano
1	teaspoon salt
½	teaspoon ground black pepper
½	teaspoon cayenne pepper

2 large baking potatoes, washed (not pared) and cut into ½-inch-thick diagonal slices

1 pound frozen boneless beef top sirloin steak, cut 1 inch thick

2 tablespoons olive oil

Additional salt, optional

Preheat the broiler. In a small bowl, combine all the Spicy Seasoning Mix ingredients; set aside. Arrange the potatoes on one half of a broiler pan(s); place the frozen steak on the other half. In a small bowl, combine the oil and 2 teaspoons of the Spicy Seasoning Mix; brush the potatoes with half of the mixture. Broil 1 side of the steak and potatoes, with the surface of the steak about 5 inches from the heat, for about 14 minutes; turn the steak and potatoes. Brush the potatoes with the remaining seasoned oil and continue broiling the steak and potatoes for 13 to 18 minutes more or until the steak is rare (140°) to medium (160°). Remove the steak to a serving platter, keeping it warm, and continue broiling the potatoes for 8 to 10 minutes more, or until tender. Season the steak and potatoes with additional salt, if desired.

NOTE: These potatoes can be made without the steak if you just want to make Spicy Potatoes. And you can make the Spicy Seasoning Mix in advance and store it in an airtight container; shake before using.

Champion Chili

about 10 servings (about 13 cups)

In the Heartland, this one's a definite winner!
(And your family'll feel like the biggest
winners when they taste this.)

2 tablespoons vegetable oil

2 medium-sized onions, diced

1 medium-sized green bell pepper, diced

1 large celery stalk, diced

2 garlic cloves, minced

4 pounds lean ground meat

1 can (4 ounces) diced green chilies

1 can (14½ ounces) stewed tomatoes

1 can (8 ounces) tomato sauce

1 can (6 ounces) tomato paste

⅔ cup (1 3-ounce bottle) chili powder

1 tablespoon ground cumin

½ teaspoon hot pepper sauce (or to taste)

6 ounces (½ of a 12-ounce can) beer

1½ cups club soda or mineral water

2 bay leaves

2 teaspoons garlic salt

½ teaspoon black pepper

In a large pot, heat the oil over medium-high heat; sauté the onions, green pepper, and celery just until soft. Add the garlic and meat; break up the meat and cook until it browns completely. Stir in the remaining ingredients. Reduce heat to low and cook for about 3 hours, stirring often. **Remove bay leaves before serving.**

NOTE: How about having this on hand with a loaf of crusty bread for your weekend at home? And it's just as nice served with cheese and crackers when company drops by.

Coney Island Hot Dogs

6 to 8 servings

Visit Coney Island and enjoy its world-famous tastes—
without leaving home.

½ pound ground beef
1 medium-sized onion, chopped
1 can (8 ounces) tomato sauce
1 teaspoon chili powder
½ teaspoon Worcestershire
 sauce

½ teaspoon dried oregano
¼ teaspoon hot pepper sauce
6 to 8 hot dogs
6 to 8 hot dog buns

In a large skillet, cook the beef and onion over medium heat, stirring often, until the beef is browned. Add the remaining ingredients, except the buns. Bring to a boil, reduce heat to low, and cook for 8 to 10 minutes or until the hot dogs are heated through. Serve the hot dogs in the buns, topped with the sauce.

Country-Fried Steak

about 3 servings

*Southern and Midwestern homestyle, all-American cooking
at its best, but this way . . . no fuss!!*

1½ pounds cubed steak	½ cup vegetable oil
½ cup Italian salad dressing	Salt to taste
½ cup all-purpose flour	Pepper to taste

Cut the cubed steak into individual-sized portions and place in a large bowl. Pour the Italian dressing over the steak pieces and toss well. Place the flour in a plastic bag or dish; add the steak pieces and coat well. In a heavy skillet, heat the oil over medium-high heat; add the steak pieces and fry, turning to brown both sides. Then fry the steak for approximately 2 minutes more per side or until a golden-brown crust has formed. Before serving, add the salt and pepper.

NOTE: Serve over mashed potatoes, if you like. You can also try this recipe with hamburger, or with chicken, turkey, or veal cutlets, instead of steak. Instead of Italian dressing, you can try your favorite salad dressing—creamy, plain, or light—and any other seasonings that will give it your own special touch.

Fifties-Style Salisbury Steak

6 servings

It's back in style . . . and better than ever!
(And still one of my favorites.)

1 can (10¾ ounces) condensed cream of mushroom soup, divided	1 teaspoon garlic powder
1 pound ground beef	½ teaspoon pepper
⅓ cup dry bread crumbs	1½ cups sliced fresh mushrooms (about 3¾ ounces)
½ cup finely chopped onion	Chopped fresh parsley for garnish (optional)
1 egg, beaten	
2 teaspoons chopped fresh parsley	

In a large bowl, thoroughly mix ¼ cup of the soup, the ground beef, bread crumbs, onion, egg, the 2 teaspoons of chopped fresh parsley, garlic powder, and pepper. Shape into firm patties. Coat a large skillet with nonstick vegetable spray. Over medium-high heat, cook half of the patties until browned on both sides. Remove from the skillet and set aside; repeat the procedure with the remaining patties. Spoon off the fat. In the same skillet, mix together the remaining soup and the mushrooms, then add the patties. Reduce the heat to low, cover, and cook, turning occasionally, for 20 minutes or until the patties are thoroughly cooked and no pink remains. Garnish with parsley and serve.

NOTE: You can substitute 1 pound ground turkey for the beef but if you do, be sure to increase the bread crumbs to ½ cup.

Honey Garlic Pork Chops

5 to 6 servings

With this tasty combination of flavors that comes from Chicago,
this is exactly the light yet full flavor we're looking for today.
And fresh from the grill . . . heaven!

MARINADE

¾ cup lemon juice

¾ cup honey

6 tablespoons soy sauce

3 tablespoons dry sherry or any
dry white wine

6 garlic cloves, chopped

10 to 12 pork chops, cut 1½
inches thick

In a glass baking dish, combine the marinade ingredients. Add the pork chops to the marinade, coating completely. Cover and refrigerate overnight to "marry" the flavors, turning once. Remove the chops from the marinade and discard the remaining marinade. Preheat the grill. Grill the chops for about 10 minutes per side or until cooked through.

NOTE: I prefer to use center-cut loin chops for a special meal, but rib chops will work just as well. And if it's not convenient to use the grill, these will cook up just fine in the broiler, too.

"Mapple" Roasted Ham

4 servings

Yum! Maple syrup **and** *apples . . . you can almost smell the fresh country air of New England at sap-gathering time.*

½ cup applesauce

3 tablespoons maple syrup

1 tablespoon prepared horseradish mustard

4 thick ham slices (½ pound per slice)

Preheat the oven to 350°F. In a small bowl, combine the applesauce, maple syrup, and mustard, stirring until well blended. Pour half of the mixture evenly over the bottom of a 9" × 13" baking dish. Place the ham slices over the mixture; pour the remaining mixture evenly over the ham. Bake for 20 to 25 minutes, or until heated through.

Marinated Steak Sandwiches

3 to 4 servings (about 1 cup marinade)

Looking for a way to be the star of the patio circuit?
This grilled sandwich always makes a hit with our
summer neighbors in Narragansett, Rhode Island.

MARINADE

3 tablespoons white wine vinegar

2 tablespoons sugar

2 tablespoons honey

1 teaspoon dry mustard

1 teaspoon salt

1 teaspoon celery seed

1 teaspoon dried tarragon, crushed

1 teaspoon onion powder

½ teaspoon pepper

½ cup olive oil

1 top round steak, cut 1 inch thick

3 or 4 toasted hoagie, torpedo, or submarine rolls

Lettuce for topping

Onion slices for topping

In a large bowl, combine all the marinade ingredients except the oil. Whisk the mixture while gradually drizzling in the olive oil until the marinade starts to thicken. Remove ⅔ cup of the marinade, cover, and refrigerate for later use. Place the remaining marinade into a resealable plastic bag; add the steak and turn to completely coat it. Refrigerate the marinating steak for 1 to 2 hours, turning steak occasionally. Remove the steak from the marinade, discarding the used marinade. Preheat the grill. Grill the steak to desired doneness, turning once and brushing it with 2 tablespoons of the reserved marinade. Slice the steak and place it on the toasted rolls, add the lettuce and onion slices, and drizzle with the remaining reserved marinade.

NOTE: If you have some garlic spread on hand, put some on the toasted rolls before adding the steak and other fixin's. Mmm . . . mmm!!

My Family's Favorite Casserole

about 4 servings

There's nothing homier or more welcoming than a hearty casserole at the end of a busy day. Here's a different one that's even better the day after—if there's any left!

¾ cup uncooked elbow macaroni

1 pound lean ground beef

½ cup sliced celery (about 2 stalks)

½ cup diced onion (about ½ of a small onion)

1 can (28 ounces) whole peeled tomatoes, broken up (undrained)

2 tablespoons honey

¼ teaspoon salt

¼ teaspoon pepper

Preheat the oven to 350°F. In a medium-sized pot of boiling salted water, cook the pasta just until tender; drain. Meanwhile, in a large skillet, brown the beef over medium-high heat; drain off the excess liquid. Combine all the ingredients in a 2-quart casserole and bake, covered, for 30 minutes. Uncover and bake for 30 minutes more or until the top is light golden and crunchy.

Onion Chili Burgers

8 servings

*Some say the West is best, and when it comes to chili burgers,
it's absolutely true!*

2½ pounds ground beef

1 envelope (from a 2-ounce box) onion or beefy onion soup mix

⅓ cup water

⅓ cup chili sauce

2 tablespoons finely chopped green bell pepper

¼ teaspoon black pepper

In a large bowl, combine all the ingredients; mix together lightly. Shape into eight ¾-inch-thick patties, and cook over a preheated barbecue grill to desired doneness. Serve on hamburger buns.

NOTE: If you want to broil these instead, that works well, too!

Ranch Beef 'n' Beans

4 to 6 servings

This is a regular on dinner tables in the Midwest.
How 'bout enjoying the goodness of
that down-home cooking?

1 pound lean ground beef

1 cup chopped onion (about ½ of a large onion)

1 can (16 ounces) kidney beans, drained

1 can (16 ounces) butter beans, drained

1 can (16 ounces) baked beans

¾ cup ketchup

1 can (4 ounces) chopped or diced mild green chilies

1 tablespoon prepared mustard

1 teaspoon beef bouillon

½ cup water

2 tablespoons honey

⅔ cup chopped green bell pepper

1 teaspoon Worcestershire sauce

½ teaspoon garlic powder

In a large skillet, brown the ground beef over medium heat until cooked through, stirring occasionally and crumbling with a fork; drain. Add the remaining ingredients and mix thoroughly. Bring to a boil, then immediately reduce the heat and simmer for 20 to 25 minutes to blend the flavors, stirring occasionally.

Rocky Mountain Lamb

2 to 3 servings

*There's nothing like our American lamb. For a change of pace,
try it this way. And talk about mouth-watering. . . !!!*

4   lamb loin chops or steaks
    (about ¼ pound each)

MARINADE

½ teaspoon black pepper

¼ teaspoon hot pepper sauce

½ teaspoon onion powder

½ teaspoon garlic powder

⅛ teaspoon freshly grated
   lemon rind

2   tablespoons olive oil

2   tablespoons water

2   tablespoons balsamic
    vinegar

1½ teaspoons dried rosemary

½ teaspoon prepared coarse-
   grained mustard

Place the lamb chops in a shallow dish. In a medium-sized bowl,
combine all the marinade ingredients. Pour the marinade over the
lamb chops, cover, and refrigerate for about 1 hour, turning once.
Remove from the marinade, discarding excess marinade, and broil
for 4 to 6 minutes per side for medium-rare, or until desired doneness.

Salted Eye of the Round Barbecue

8 to 10 servings (¼ to ½ pound per person)

This is a particular method of cooking eye of the round where the
meat is cooked directly on barbecue coals or on the lava
rocks of a gas grill. You need to follow the directions
carefully and give it your complete attention, but
boy, oh boy, is it ever worth it! (Believe me,
they'll be amazed when they see you do this.)

1 eye of the round roast   4 cups kosher (coarse) salt

Heat a charcoal grill and let it burn until there is a good bed of red-hot coals, or remove the grate from a gas grill and set the heat to high. Meanwhile, tear off a piece of waxed paper large enough to completely wrap the roast. (Use two sheets, if necessary, and over-lap them.) Place the waxed paper flat on a countertop, place the roast in the center, and pour the kosher salt over the meat. Use your clean hands to spread the salt evenly over both sides of the meat until it is completely covered and white. DO NOT BE AFRAID TO USE TOO MUCH SALT. Wrap the meat as completely as you can so that all of the salt stays inside the wrapper.

HERE'S WHERE YOU NEED TO BE CAREFUL: Place the waxed paper–wrapped meat directly on the hot coals or lava rocks and STAND BACK IMMEDIATELY, as the waxed paper will immedi-ately flame up and burn away. Leave the grill cover off. Let the meat cook for 35 to 40 minutes on one side, then use two long-handled meat forks or long-handled tongs to flip the meat, and cook for 30 to 35 minutes more on the second side. Again, DO NOT COVER THE GRILL. And again, BE CAREFUL!!

Carefully remove the meat from the coals and scrape off any re-maining bits of waxed paper and salt. (The outside of the meat will be black.) Place the meat in something shallow for carving, so that the juices can be saved for serving over it. Carve across the roast the short way in thin (about ¼-inch) slices.

NOTE: If directions are followed carefully, you'll end up with a range of slices from medium rare to well done, so that everybody can have moist and delicious roast beef done their own perfect way. Please be sure to keep children away from your fire.

San Antonio Burgers

6 servings

*The next time you do burgers, why not give them a real
flavor boost? They'll be a sure hit!*

1½	pounds lean ground beef	1	egg
1	cup picante sauce, plus extra for topping	1	teaspoon salt
¾	cup quick oats, uncooked	¼	teaspoon pepper
1	small onion, chopped	1	teaspoon chili powder
		6	hamburger buns

Preheat the grill or broiler. In a large bowl, combine all the ingredients except the buns; mix together well. Shape into 6 large patties. Grill or broil to desired doneness. Serve on buns with additional picante sauce.

Sausage Gravy and Biscuits

6 to 8 servings

*There's nothing quite like the aroma of freshly baked biscuits to
make us feel at-home comfortable. And served with sausage
gravy—oh, oh, what a treat! Even though the entire South can take
credit for them, I especially loved the ones I had in Alexandria,
Louisiana. (And I confess—most times I use biscuit mix
so I can get to the gravy faster!)*

SAUSAGE GRAVY

2 pounds bulk breakfast sausage (not links)

1 cup chopped onion

6 tablespoons all-purpose flour

3 cups milk

⅛ teaspoon pepper

In a large skillet, brown the sausage and onion over medium
heat, stirring with a fork to break up chunks of meat; drain off liquid.
Sprinkle the flour over the sausage mixture, stirring to coat the meat.
Reduce heat to low, cook and stir for 1 to 2 minutes; do not allow
the flour to brown. Slowly stir in the milk, cooking and stirring until
the mixture thickens and boils. Stir in the pepper and simmer for 5
minutes. Serve over store-bought biscuits or make your own using
the recipe on page 136.

NOTE: For a thinner consistency, more milk may be needed.

Biscuits

about 12

2¼ cups all-purpose flour plus extra for working the dough

4 teaspoons baking powder

½ teaspoon baking soda

½ teaspoon salt

1 tablespoon sugar

¼ cup butter-flavored or other shortening

2 tablespoons cold butter, cut into 6 equal pieces

¾ cup buttermilk

Preheat the oven to 450°F. In a medium-sized bowl, sift together the flour, baking powder, baking soda, salt, and sugar. Cut in the shortening and butter, using a fork or pastry cutter, until the mixture resembles coarse crumbs. Stir in the buttermilk, mixing just until the dry ingredients are moistened. Let the dough sit for 1 minute, then transfer it to a lightly floured work surface. Lightly dust the top of the dough with flour and roll out to ½-inch thickness with a rolling pin. Cut out the biscuits with a 2-inch cutter (dip the cutter in flour before cutting each biscuit, to prevent sticking). Place the biscuits on ungreased baking sheets and bake for 10 to 12 minutes, or just until they begin to turn golden. Remove from the baking sheets and serve warm.

Sloppy Joes

4 to 6 servings

*An American favorite, for sure! C'mon, what family doesn't
have a Sloppy Joe night? After all, it's the one meal
the kids (and all of us) really love.*

2 pounds ground beef or veal	¼ teaspoon black pepper
1 can (10¾ ounces) tomato soup	¼ teaspoon garlic powder
	½ teaspoon hot pepper sauce
¼ cup water	¼ cup ketchup
2 teaspoons dried oregano	1 teaspoon chili powder
2 teaspoons Worcestershire sauce	4 to 6 hamburger buns, split and toasted

In a large skillet, cook the beef over medium heat until browned, stirring occasionally to break up the meat. Spoon off the fat. Add all the remaining ingredients, except the buns; cook for 3 to 5 minutes, stirring frequently. Serve on the toasted buns.

Steak Salad

about 4 servings

Here are the lively tastes of the Southwest in a smart salad—
and we're finding this great combination in
today's trendy restaurants, too.

1 cup ranch salad dressing (1 8-ounce bottle)

¼ cup picante sauce

1 tablespoon taco seasoning mix

1½ pounds well-trimmed boneless beef top sirloin steak, cut 1 inch thick

3 cups torn red or green leaf lettuce

3 cups torn fresh spinach leaves

1 small red or white onion, thinly sliced and separated into rings

Salt to taste

Freshly ground black pepper to taste

1 large tomato, seeded and chopped

1 medium-sized red bell pepper, chopped

In a small bowl, combine the salad dressing, picante sauce, and taco seasoning mix; cover and refrigerate. Grill or broil the steak to desired doneness. While the steak is cooking, place the lettuce and spinach on a serving platter and top with the onion slices. Let the steak stand for 10 minutes, then carve the steak diagonally across the grain into thin slices. Sprinkle with salt and pepper, as desired. Arrange the steak strips over the vegetables; drizzle with a small amount of the dressing mixture. Sprinkle the chopped tomato and red pepper over the salad. Serve with the remaining dressing.

Thirty-Minute Beef Chili

4 servings

*They say there's no better chili than in Texas, but now we can
have those same Texas flavors wherever we live. I must
admit that I added the tomatoes myself. You see, true
Texas chili doesn't ever have tomatoes (or beans,
either), but after you taste this I'm sure
you'll forgive me.*

1	pound lean beef cubed steaks	½	teaspoon salt
4½	teaspoons Texas Seasoning Mix, divided (see recipe below)	1	can (28 ounces) whole tomatoes, undrained
2	teaspoons vegetable oil	1	box (9 ounces) frozen whole-kernel corn, thawed
1	medium-sized onion, chopped		

Cut each beef steak lengthwise into 1-inch-wide strips; cut crosswise into 1-inch pieces. Sprinkle the beef with 2 teaspoons Texas Seasoning Mix. Heat the oil in a large deep skillet over medium heat. Stir-fry the beef and onion for 2 to 3 minutes. Season with the salt. Add the tomatoes (break them up with the back of a spoon), corn, and the remaining 2½ teaspoons Texas Seasoning Mix. Bring to a boil, then reduce heat to medium-low and simmer, uncovered, for 18 to 20 minutes.

Texas Seasoning Mix

about ⅓ cup

3	tablespoons chili powder	¾	teaspoon dried oregano
2	teaspoons ground cumin	½	teaspoon cayenne pepper
1½	teaspoons garlic powder		

Combine all the ingredients in a small bowl. Store, covered, in an airtight container until ready to use. Shake to blend before using.

Twist Pasta with Pork and Pepper Sauce

4 to 6 servings

*Here's a tasty treat with an exciting "twist"! And the meat
is so tender, it melts in your mouth.*

3 tablespoons olive oil, divided	2 garlic cloves, finely chopped
½ of a green bell pepper, cut into strips	1 jar (25 to 29 ounces) spaghetti sauce
½ of a red bell pepper, cut into strips	¼ teaspoon dried thyme leaves, crushed
1 medium-sized onion, cut into eighths	½ pound twist pasta or any medium pasta shape
¾ to 1 pound pork tenderloin, cut into ½-inch cubes	

In a large skillet, heat the oil over medium-high heat; add the peppers and onion and cook until tender-crisp, about 4 minutes. Remove the peppers and onion from the skillet and set aside; add the pork and garlic to the skillet and cook over high heat until the pork is browned. Add the spaghetti sauce and thyme, reduce the heat to low, and simmer, uncovered, for 20 minutes or until the pork is tender, stirring occasionally; add the cooked vegetables. Meanwhile, in a large pot of boiling salted water, cook the pasta to desired doneness; drain and place in a large bowl. Toss the pasta with the remaining tablespoon of oil. Serve with the pork and pepper sauce.

Fish and Seafood

Baked Halibut

4 to 5 servings

*Seafood is a mainstay of the American Northwest
and, chances are, this recipe will become
a mainstay in your kitchen!*

1 cup bottled barbecue sauce	4 or 5 halibut steaks
2 tablespoons olive oil	¼ cup seasoned bread crumbs
½ teaspoon onion powder	2 tablespoons grated Parmesan cheese
¼ teaspoon garlic powder	

Preheat the oven to 375°F. In a small saucepan, combine the barbecue sauce, olive oil, and onion and garlic powders over low heat; simmer for 2 minutes or until heated through. Keep warm. Place the halibut steaks in a greased 9" × 13" baking pan. Pour half of the barbecue sauce mixture over the halibut steaks, then brush to evenly distribute. In a small bowl, combine the bread crumbs and Parmesan cheese; sprinkle over the halibut. Bake for 15 to 20 minutes or until the fish becomes firm and flakes easily with a fork. Warm the remaining barbecue sauce mixture and serve with the baked fish.

NOTE: Cook fish for about 10 minutes per inch of thickness; that way it'll stay moist.

Campfire Rainbow Trout Fillets

4 servings

It doesn't matter whether you're all in the kitchen, the backyard,
or by a mountain stream, they'll think they're sitting under
the stars listening to the crackle of the campfire
when you serve this!

½   cup all-purpose flour
1½ teaspoons paprika
1   teaspoon ground thyme
¼   teaspoon salt
⅛   teaspoon pepper

1 egg, beaten
4 fresh or frozen trout fillets
   (about 4 ounces each), thawed
   if frozen
1 tablespoon olive oil

In a shallow bowl, combine the flour, paprika, thyme, salt, and pepper; set aside. Place the beaten egg in another shallow bowl. Dip the trout fillets in the egg, then dredge in the flour mixture. In a large skillet, heat the oil over medium-high heat; sauté the fillets for 1 to 2 minutes per side, or until the fish flakes easily with a fork.

NOTE: For a different taste treat, I sometimes add a tablespoon of cornmeal to the flour mixture.

Cioppino

2 to 3 servings

Thank you, San Francisco, for this delectable creation!

1 tablespoon olive oil

1 bunch scallions, cut into
¼-inch slices

2 tablespoons chopped fresh
parsley

2 garlic cloves, chopped

1 can (8 ounces) tomato sauce

¾ cup to 1 cup dry white wine

⅛ teaspoon salt

⅛ teaspoon pepper

About 1 pound white-fleshed fish
fillets (cod, haddock, or sole)

In a large skillet, heat the oil over medium-high heat; add the scallions, parsley, and garlic. Sauté for about 2 minutes, then add the tomato sauce, wine, salt, and pepper. Reduce heat and simmer, uncovered, for about 12 minutes. Meanwhile, wash the fish fillets and pat dry. Place them in the sauce in a single layer. Simmer, partially covered, for 7 to 8 minutes, then turn the fish and continue simmering for another 8 to 10 minutes, or until the fish flakes easily with a fork.

NOTE: Cooking times may vary, depending on the thickness of the fish. Serve this in a bowl with traditional San Francisco sourdough bread or any other crispy bread so you can sop up the juices. Mmmm!!

Cod Cakes

10 to 12 patties

*Your family will feel like they've been transported
to the Cape for dinner! Not a bad trick, eh?*

2   cups steamed cod (about 1
    pound fresh)
2   cups mashed potatoes
1   large onion, minced
1   egg, well beaten
½   cup bread crumbs
2   tablespoons mayonnaise

½   teaspoon salt
2   teaspoons seafood seasoning
½   teaspoon dried thyme
⅛   teaspoon pepper
¼   teaspoon ground nutmeg
1   cup cornflake crumbs

Preheat the oven to 400°F. In a large bowl, break the fish apart and mash with the remaining ingredients, except the cornflake crumbs. Place the cornflake crumbs in a shallow dish. Form the fish into patties; coat the patties evenly on both sides with the crumbs. Place on a cookie sheet that has been coated with nonstick vegetable spray and bake for 15 minutes, or until warmed through.

NOTE: You can use instant potato flakes instead of real mashed potatoes. They work just as well.

Crab-Stuffed Sole

2 servings

I've had this in cities all along the East Coast, and one of the best recipes is this one from one of my favorite cities, Savannah, Georgia.

1 can (4 ounces) mushrooms, drained

1 can (6 ounces) flaked crabmeat, drained

¼ cup (½ stick) butter, melted

¼ teaspoon salt

¼ teaspoon pepper

⅔ cup cracker crumbs

2 tablespoons dry sherry

4 medium-sized sole or flounder fillets (about 1 pound)

2 tablespoons butter for dotting

Preheat the oven to 350°F. In a large bowl, combine the mushrooms, crabmeat, melted butter, salt, pepper, cracker crumbs, and sherry. Place 2 fish fillets in a 9" × 13" baking dish that has been coated with nonstick vegetable spray; divide the crabmeat mixture and spread evenly over the 2 fillets, then cover with the 2 remaining fillets. Dot with the butter. Bake for 30 minutes or until the fish flakes easily with a fork.

NOTE: In a pinch, an 8-ounce package of imitation crabmeat will work for the canned.

Fish Gumbo

about 6 servings

*When we hear "gumbo," we automatically think of Louisiana
'cause it started there and that's where they make it best!
Here's a nice one that's easy enough for us.*

1   cup chopped onion
1   cup thinly sliced celery
¾   cup chopped green bell
     pepper
1   tablespoon finely chopped
     fresh parsley, plus extra for
     garnish
1   garlic clove, minced
¼   cup (½ stick) butter
1   tablespoon all-purpose flour
1½   teaspoons chili powder
1½   teaspoons salt
1   teaspoon paprika
⅛   teaspoon cayenne pepper

½   teaspoon Cajun seasoning
1   can (14½ ounces) tomatoes,
     undrained, broken up
1   can (8 ounces) tomato sauce
½   cup water
1   pound fresh or frozen fish
     fillets, skinned and cut into
     1½-inch pieces (thaw if
     frozen)
1   package (10 ounces) frozen
     whole okra, thawed, or 1 can
     (14¼ ounces), drained
2   cups hot cooked rice

In a soup pot over medium heat, cook the onion, celery, green
pepper, 1 tablespoon parsley, and garlic in the butter until the vegetables are tender but not brown, stirring occasionally. In a small
bowl, combine the flour, chili powder, salt, paprika, cayenne pepper, and Cajun seasoning; stir into the vegetables. Add the tomatoes,
tomato sauce, and water; simmer for 4 to 6 minutes. Add the fish
and okra; reduce the heat, cover, and simmer for 10 to 15 minutes
more or until the fish flakes easily with a fork and the okra is tender.

NOTE: Serve with hot cooked rice and garnish with chopped parsley.
For a hotter taste, double the Cajun seasoning.

Mardi Gras Shrimp

4 to 6 servings

Here's another taste of New Orleans cooking—with those special authentic flavors . . . but without the traditional work or mess!

¼ cup (½ stick) butter
1 medium-sized onion, chopped
1 garlic clove, minced
½ of a green bell pepper, finely chopped
1 teaspoon salt
Pinch of black pepper
1 can (14½ ounces) tomatoes, undrained, broken up
1 pound cleaned cooked shrimp
2 cups hot cooked rice

In a large skillet, melt the butter over medium heat; add the onion, garlic, green pepper, salt, black pepper, and tomatoes. Reduce heat to low and simmer for 15 minutes, stirring occasionally. Add the shrimp; continue heating until the shrimp are warm, about 3 minutes. Serve over the rice.

NOTE: For some variety, why not try adding some hot pepper sauce for a zing, or fresh tomatoes, basil, thyme, or zucchini—do whatever you like!

New England Cheesy Crab Melt

8 open-faced sandwiches

A sandwich popular with fishermen and landlubbers from coast to coast.

4 kaiser or hard rolls, split
¼ cup mayonnaise
2 tablespoons Dijon-style mustard
8 ounces cooked crabmeat or imitation crab

1 package (10 ounces) frozen asparagus pieces, thawed and drained
6 ounces sliced mozzarella cheese
Paprika for sprinkling

Preheat the broiler. Place the roll halves, cut side up, on a broiler pan. Broil 5 inches from the heat for about 45 seconds or until toasted. In a small bowl, combine the mayonnaise and mustard; spread on each toasted roll half. Divide the crabmeat and asparagus evenly among the roll halves. Place ½ a slice of cheese on top of each; sprinkle with paprika. Broil for 1 minute or until the cheese is melted. Turn off the broiler; keep the sandwiches in the hot broiler for 3 to 5 minutes, until hot and bubbly.

Oven-"Fried" Fish

about 4 servings

So crispy and crunchy, they'll swear it's fried—and then they'll swear it's delicious . . . which, of course, it is!

2 pounds cod or haddock fillets
1 egg, beaten
1 tablespoon vegetable oil
¼ teaspoon salt
¼ teaspoon pepper
¼ teaspoon dried dillweed
¼ teaspoon paprika
¼ teaspoon garlic powder
1 cup fine cornflake crumbs

Preheat the oven to 400°F. Cut each fillet into 3-inch-wide pieces. In a shallow dish, combine the egg, oil, salt, pepper, dillweed, paprika, and garlic powder. Place the cornflake crumbs in a separate shallow dish. Dip the fish pieces into the egg mixture, then in the cornflakes. Place on a baking pan that has been coated with nonstick vegetable spray and bake for 20 to 25 minutes, or until the fish flakes easily with a fork.

Rhode Island Tuna Steaks

about 4 servings

Fresh tuna steaks let you be the hit of the night with the catch of the day! (And did you know that Point Judith, Rhode Island, is the Tuna Capital of the World?!)

MARINADE

1 cup dry red wine
1 cup soy sauce
1 teaspoon ground ginger
2 tablespoons honey
1 teaspoon hot pepper sauce
½ teaspoon garlic powder
4 teaspoons sugar

2 pounds tuna steak

Preheat the oven to 350°F. In a small bowl, mix together all the marinade ingredients. Place the tuna in a 9" × 13" baking dish and pour the prepared marinade over the tuna. Marinate, uncovered, in the refrigerator for 10 minutes. Pour off and discard the marinade, leaving just enough to cover the bottom of the baking dish. Bake for 15 to 20 minutes, or until the fish flakes easily with a fork.

San Diego Catch

4 servings

You sure won't have to fish for compliments when you put this on the dinner table. (Make extra . . . 'cause every time I make it, I can't stop eating it!)

½	cup cornmeal	1	egg, lightly beaten
2	teaspoons chili powder	1	pound fish fillets
1	teaspoon salt	¼	cup vegetable oil
¼	teaspoon pepper		

In a shallow dish, combine the cornmeal, chili powder, salt, and pepper. Place the beaten egg in another shallow dish. Dip the fish in the egg, then dredge in the cornmeal mixture; shake off the excess. In a large skillet, heat the vegetable oil over medium-high heat until hot. Add the fish and sauté until lightly browned on both sides, 3 to 4 minutes. Drain on paper towels before serving.

NOTE: Flounder and sole work well here. And, for a special treat, orange roughy prepared this way is out of this world!

Shrimp Étouffé

4 servings

*A Louisiana friend shared her recipe with me, and I've
come up with a few shortcuts. What a simple way
to take a trip to America's fine food center.*

2 tablespoons vegetable oil
1 medium-sized onion, chopped
1 medium-sized green bell
  pepper, chopped
⅛ teaspoon black pepper
1 jar (16 ounces) medium
  chunky salsa

2 cans (4¼ ounces each) broken
  shrimp, undrained
1 can (10½ ounces) chicken
  broth

In a large skillet, heat the oil over medium heat; add the onion
and green pepper and sauté until tender, about 5 minutes. Add the
remaining ingredients, reduce the heat, and simmer for 30 minutes,
stirring occasionally.

NOTE: Serve over hot cooked rice. For a true New Orleans taste, add
one 14½-ounce can of okra after sautéing the veggies.

Sole with Mushrooms

3 to 4 servings

Go ahead, impress the family with this classy coastal dish.

4 sole fillets (about 4 ounces each)

½ teaspoon salt

¼ teaspoon pepper

1 cup sliced fresh mushrooms

1 medium-sized tomato, seeded and chopped

½ cup (2 ounces) shredded mozzarella cheese

2 tablespoons grated Parmesan cheese

Preheat the oven to 325°F. Place the fillets in a lightly greased 7" × 11" baking dish. Sprinkle the salt, pepper, mushrooms, and tomatoes over the fillets. Cover and bake for 20 to 25 minutes or until the fish flakes easily with a fork. Uncover and sprinkle with the mozzarella and Parmesan cheeses. Cover and let stand for about 3 minutes or until cheeses are melted.

Sour Cream Fish

about 4 servings

This is a no-fail easy way to put some
fish excitement on your table!

2 pounds sole or other white-
  fleshed fish fillets
1 cup sour cream
1 teaspoon salt
½ teaspoon hot pepper sauce

1 tablespoon paprika
¼ cup grated Parmesan cheese
1 tablespoon bread crumbs
Butter or margarine for dotting

Preheat the oven to 350°F. Arrange the fish fillets in a 9" × 13" baking dish that has been coated with nonstick vegetable spray; set aside. In a medium-sized bowl, combine the sour cream, salt, hot pepper sauce, paprika, and Parmesan cheese. Spread the mixture over the fish. Top with the bread crumbs and dot with butter. Bake, uncovered, for about 20 minutes, or until the fish flakes easily with a fork.

Tuna and Corn Skillet

4 servings (about 4 cups)

*Wow!! Here's a rich, robust one-pot meal that's easy to prepare
and even easier to enjoy! And it's a fish dish that
joins the best of the Coast and the Heartland.*

2   to 3 tablespoons butter
1   small onion, chopped
1   can (10¾ ounces) cream of
    shrimp soup
½   cup milk

1   can (17 ounces) whole-kernel
    corn, drained
1   can (12¼ ounces) tuna,
    drained and flaked
¼   teaspoon pepper

In a large skillet, melt the butter over medium heat; add the onion and sauté until tender and translucent, about 2 to 3 minutes. Stir in the soup and milk. Add the corn, tuna, and pepper; heat through, stirring occasionally.

NOTE: Serve over hot cooked rice. With a side salad and hot rolls, it's a great quick meal.

Wined and Dined Cod

4 to 6 servings

*This simple but elegant dish comes straight from
the New England coast.*

MARINADE

2 tablespoons lemon juice

6 tablespoons dry white wine

2 tablespoons olive oil

2 teaspoons sugar

2 tablespoons finely chopped onion

½ teaspoon salt

¼ teaspoon dried dillweed

¼ teaspoon hot pepper sauce

6 cod or other white-fleshed fish fillets (4 to 5 ounces each)

Dash of black pepper, optional

Dash of paprika, optional

In a large bowl, combine all the marinade ingredients. Add the fish, cover, and marinate in the refrigerator for 2 to 3 hours. Preheat the oven to 350°F. Remove the fish from the marinade, discarding excess marinade. Place the fillets in a 9" × 13" baking pan that has been coated with nonstick vegetable spray and sprinkle with black pepper and paprika, if desired. Bake for 15 to 20 minutes or until the fish flakes easily with a fork.

Potatoes and Rice

Black Bean and Rice Salad

about 3½ cups

*Boy, do those Louisianans know how to do flavor! For instance,
their black beans and rice . . . Well, here's a shortcut way to
that flavor in a salad that fits inside, outside, winter,
summer, and everything in between.*

2 cups cooked rice, cooled to room temperature

1 cup canned black beans, drained

1 cup chopped fresh tomato

½ cup (2 ounces) shredded Cheddar cheese (optional)

1 tablespoon chopped fresh parsley

¼ cup prepared Italian dressing

1 tablespoon fresh lime juice

In a large bowl, combine the rice, beans, tomato, cheese, and parsley. Pour the dressing and lime juice over the rice mixture; toss well and serve.

Country Potatoes

4 servings

A real country breakfast wouldn't be complete without these.
(For lunch or dinner they wouldn't hurt, either!)

2 teaspoons butter, melted
2 tablespoons water, divided
2 teaspoons parsley flakes
⅛ teaspoon paprika
¼ teaspoon salt
¼ teaspoon pepper

¼ teaspoon dried dillweed
1 pound new potatoes, cut into thin slices (2 to 3 medium-sized potatoes)
1 onion, chopped

In a medium-sized bowl, combine the melted butter, 1 tablespoon water, parsley, paprika, salt, pepper, and dillweed. Add the potatoes and toss to coat. In a large skillet that has been coated with nonstick vegetable spray, sauté the potatoes and onion until tender, 8 to 10 minutes. Add the remaining 1 tablespoon water after the first 4 minutes, or when the potatoes first start to stick to the skillet.

Cranberry Candied Yams

4 servings

*Cranberries from the Northeast and sweet potatoes from the South—
now that's an all-American dish that everybody can agree on!*

4   medium-sized yams or sweet
    potatoes
½ cup whole-berry cranberry
    sauce

3   tablespoons lemon juice
⅓ cup honey
1   tablespoon melted butter

In a large saucepan, cook the potatoes in boiling water until just tender. Preheat the oven to 350°F. Cool the potatoes slightly, then peel, split lengthwise, and place in a greased 8-inch square baking dish. In a small bowl, combine the cranberry sauce and lemon juice; spread over the potatoes. Then, in the same bowl, combine the honey and butter; pour over the potatoes. Bake for 25 minutes, basting occasionally.

NOTE: If you don't have fresh yams, plain canned sweet potatoes (not ones in syrup) will work just as well. (And that way, you can skip the boiling process described above.)

Herbed Walnut Rice

4 to 6 servings

Just when we thought we'd tried every way imaginable to serve rice, we found a special way that cooks serve it in the Mountain States. It sure satisfies!

1 tablespoon butter	¼ teaspoon dried thyme leaves
½ cup chopped onion	⅛ teaspoon dried rosemary
½ cup shredded carrot	3 cups cooked rice (cooked in chicken broth)
½ cup chopped walnuts	2 tablespoons chopped fresh parsley
¼ teaspoon dried marjoram	

In a large skillet, melt the butter over medium-high heat; add the onion, carrot, walnuts, marjoram, thyme, and rosemary and cook until the vegetables are tender-crisp, 6 to 8 minutes. Stir in the rice and parsley; heat thoroughly.

Holiday Potatoes

10 to 12 servings

Why "holiday"? Because the taste is something to celebrate!

1   bag (32 ounces) frozen hash brown potatoes, thawed

1½ cups grated Cheddar cheese, divided

1   can (10¾ ounces) cream of chicken soup

1   can (10¾ ounces) cream of celery soup

½   cup chopped onion

½   cup sour cream

2   tablespoons melted butter

Paprika for sprinkling

Preheat the oven to 350°F. In a large bowl, mix together the potatoes, 1 cup of the Cheddar cheese, the soups, onion, sour cream, and melted butter. Pour the mixture into a greased 9" × 13" baking pan. Bake for 1 hour, or until bubbly. Carefully remove from the oven and sprinkle with the remaining ½ cup Cheddar cheese and the paprika. Bake for 10 minutes more.

Home-Fried Fresh Yams

4 to 5 servings

The South is famous for these. Try some . . . they go with everything.

4 tablespoons vegetable oil

About 2½ pounds yams or sweet
   potatoes, peeled and cut into
   ¼-inch-thick slices (2 to 3
   large yams)

¼ teaspoon salt

In a large skillet, heat the oil over medium-high heat; add the potatoes and fry for 10 to 15 minutes, turning occasionally until brown and crisp. Season with the salt.

Homestyle Mashed Potatoes

6 to 8 servings

*Here's New York style with the perfect touch of home.
Thank you, New York!*

1 pound potatoes, cut into chunks	1 teaspoon chopped garlic
1 large onion, chopped	½ teaspoon salt
1 cup chicken broth	¼ teaspoon pepper
2 tablespoons butter	1 cup frozen peas, thawed

Place the potatoes and onion in a large pot, add enough water to cover, and bring to a boil; boil until the potatoes are tender, about 25 minutes, then drain. Return the potatoes and onion to the pot, and mash with the chicken broth, butter, garlic, salt, and pepper, leaving some potato lumps! Heat the peas a bit in the microwave or on the stove, then add to the potatoes, mix lightly, and serve.

NOTE: How 'bout adding a little nutmeg or grated cheese for a different taste treat? Try adding your own touches!

Not-So-Skinny Mashed Potatoes

about 6 servings

If you're counting calories and fat, you might want to skip this one.
But they're so scrumptious, I couldn't wait to share this good
old American recipe.

2 pounds potatoes, peeled and quartered

¼ cup (½ stick) butter

1 package (8 ounces) cream cheese

1 container (8 ounces) sour cream

¼ to ½ cup reserved potato cooking water

Salt to taste

Pepper to taste

Place the potato pieces in a large pot, adding enough water to cover; heat to boiling. Reduce heat to medium and cook for 25 to 30 minutes or until the potatoes are tender. Drain the potatoes, reserving ¼ to ½ cup of the cooking water; place the potatoes in a large bowl. Cut the butter and cream cheese into small pieces and add to the potatoes, along with the sour cream and ¼ cup of the reserved potato cooking water. Beat with an electric mixer or potato masher until light and fluffy, adding more of the reserved potato water if needed to reach desired consistency. Season with the salt and pepper. Serve immediately.

Perfect Mashed Potatoes

4 to 6 servings

Everyone thinks of meat and potatoes as the all-American meal.
Well, the potato secret's out: It's the water! Read on . . .

2   pounds potatoes, peeled and
    quartered
¼ to ½ cup reserved potato
    cooking water

¼ cup (½ stick) butter
Salt to taste
Pepper to taste

Place the potato pieces in a large pot, adding enough water to
cover; heat to boiling. Reduce heat to medium and cook for 25 to
30 minutes or until the potatoes are tender. Drain the potatoes,
reserving ¼ to ½ cup of the cooking water; place the potatoes in a
large bowl. Beat with an electric mixer or potato masher until
smooth. Add the butter, salt, pepper, and ¼ cup of the reserved
potato cooking water. Continue beating until light and fluffy, adding
more of the reserved potato water if needed to reach desired consistency. Serve immediately.

Rice Ambrosia

8½ cups

*A heavenly treat that'll have them coming back for seconds
(and thirds)! And it's so easy,
and so exotic and mellow.*

½   pint heavy cream

2   cups cooked rice, cooled

3½   ounces (½ of a 7-ounce jar)
marshmallow creme,
softened

1   can (8 ounces) crushed
pineapple, drained

1   can (11 ounces) mandarin
oranges, drained

¼   cup sweetened flaked coconut

Maraschino cherries for garnish

In a medium-sized bowl, whip the heavy cream with an electric mixer until thick and fluffy; fold in the remaining ingredients except the cherries. Chill for at least 2 hours before serving. Serve in individual bowls, garnished with the cherries.

NOTE: Before using, soften the marshmallow creme slightly in the microwave.

Rice and Asparagus Casserole

8 servings

A great full-flavored side dish like they dish up at the fanciest restaurants. Now you can make it at home!

2 pounds fresh asparagus, cleaned, trimmed, and cut into 1-inch pieces
2 cups cooked rice, cooled
¼ teaspoon salt
¼ teaspoon cayenne pepper
⅓ cup sour cream
⅔ cup milk
2 cups (8 ounces) shredded sharp Cheddar cheese, divided

Preheat the oven to 350°F. In a large pot of boiling water, cook the asparagus until tender-crisp, about 10 minutes. In a medium-sized bowl, combine the rice, salt, cayenne pepper, sour cream, milk, and 1 cup of the cheese. Spoon half of the rice mixture into a 9-inch-square baking pan that has been coated with nonstick vegetable spray. Arrange the asparagus on top, then spread the remaining rice mixture over the asparagus. Bake for 20 minutes. Sprinkle the remaining cheese over the top and bake for 5 minutes more.

Rice Primavera

about 6 servings

*No, Primavera doesn't have to be pasta. It's a super hero-maker
this way . . . wait'll you see!*

2   teaspoons olive oil
1   garlic clove, minced
2   cups broccoli florets
1   cup sliced zucchini (about ½
    of a medium-sized zucchini)
1   cup sliced mushrooms (about
    2½ ounces)
1   medium-sized tomato, seeded
    and chopped

¼   cup chopped fresh parsley
⅓   cup mayonnaise
½   cup milk
¼   cup grated Parmesan cheese
¼   teaspoon pepper
3   cups cooked rice

In a large skillet, heat the oil over medium-high heat; sauté the garlic, then add the broccoli, zucchini, and mushrooms and cook until almost tender-crisp, 3 to 5 minutes. Add the tomato and parsley and cook for 1 minute more. Remove the vegetables and set aside. Add the mayonnaise to the same skillet; stir in the milk, cheese, and pepper. Cook over medium heat, stirring until smooth. Add the rice; toss to coat. Return the cooked vegetables to the skillet and heat through. Serve immediately.

Roasted Potato Salad

6 to 8 servings

When we think "potato" we naturally think "Idaho." Well,
here's a bit of Idaho in every yummy bite!

3	pounds small red or white potatoes	2	teaspoons finely chopped fresh parsley
⅓	cup olive oil	1	teaspoon grated lemon peel
1½ to 2	tablespoons fresh lemon juice	1	teaspoon crushed garlic
1½ to 2	tablespoons white wine vinegar	½	teaspoon seasoned salt
2	teaspoons dried dillweed	½	teaspoon black pepper
		¼	teaspoon hot pepper sauce
		1½	cups (6 ounces) shredded Cheddar cheese

Place the potatoes in a large pot; add enough salted water to cover, and bring to a boil. Cook the potatoes for about 20 minutes or until tender but firm. Meanwhile, combine the remaining ingredients, except the cheese, in a 9" × 13" baking pan that has been coated with nonstick vegetable spray. Drain the potatoes well, then slice them in half and add to the baking pan; toss with the oil mixture. Let stand at room temperature for 1 hour, stirring occasionally. Preheat the oven to 375°F. Bake the potatoes for 25 minutes, then sprinkle with the Cheddar cheese and bake for 5 minutes more or until the cheese is melted.

Santa Fe Rice Salad

4 to 5 servings

Delicious **and** *healthy?! You've got it! (Okay, so while they're gobbling it up, don't tell them about the healthy part!)*

2 cups cooked rice, cooled

1 can (15 ounces) black beans or pinto beans, rinsed and drained (about 1½ cups)

1 can (17 ounces) whole-kernel corn, drained (about 1½ cups)

¼ cup minced onion

2 tablespoons white vinegar

2 tablespoons vegetable oil

2 tablespoons chopped fresh parsley

1 to 2 jalapeño peppers, minced

2 teaspoons chili powder

1 teaspoon salt

¼ teaspoon sugar

In a small bowl, combine the rice, beans, corn, and onion. In another small bowl, whisk together the remaining ingredients; pour over the rice mixture. Mix well. Cover and chill for 2 to 3 hours to allow the flavors to blend. Stir before serving.

Southwest Rice Salad

4 servings (about 3½ cups)

A winner, full of color and crunch!

2 tablespoons white wine vinegar

1 teaspoon olive oil

2 to 3 drops hot pepper sauce (optional)

1 garlic clove, minced

¼ teaspoon salt

¼ teaspoon ground white pepper

2½ cups cooked rice (cooked in chicken broth), cooled to room temperature

½ cup diced red bell pepper (about ½ of a medium-sized pepper)

½ cup diced green bell pepper (about ½ of a medium-sized pepper)

¼ cup sliced scallions

¼ cup sliced black olives

In a large bowl, combine the vinegar, oil, hot pepper sauce, garlic, salt, and white pepper; mix well. Add the remaining ingredients, and toss lightly.

Sweet Potato and Pear Casserole

about 6 servings

Talk about scrumptious! There aren't enough m's in "Mmm" to describe this autumn favorite! (Although with so much of today's produce available almost year-round, it fits in any season.)

4   medium-sized sweet potatoes, peeled, cooked, and mashed

¼ cup (½ stick) melted butter, divided

3   tablespoons brown sugar

¼ teaspoon salt

¼ teaspoon ground cinnamon

2   tablespoons honey

1   teaspoon grated orange peel

1   can (16 ounces) pear halves, syrup reserved

Preheat the oven to 350°F. In a greased 1½-quart baking dish, combine the potatoes, 3 tablespoons melted butter, brown sugar, salt, and cinnamon. In a medium-sized saucepan, blend the honey, the remaining 1 tablespoon butter, orange peel, and 3 tablespoons of the reserved pear syrup; bring to a boil. Arrange the pear halves over the potato mixture, then pour the honey mixture over. Bake for 30 to 35 minutes or until golden.

Texas Broccoli and Rice Casserole

8 to 10 servings

*Bet you didn't know that the Lone Star State produces both
broccoli and rice. Well, it does—and when we put
them together so easily . . . WOW!!*

¾ cup chopped celery

¾ cup minced onion

½ cup (1 stick) butter

1 package (10 ounces) frozen
chopped broccoli, thawed and
drained

1 can (10¾ ounces) cream of
mushroom soup

1 cup chicken broth

1 cup (4 ounces) shredded
Cheddar cheese

3 cups cooked rice

Paprika for sprinkling

Preheat the oven to 350°F. In a large skillet over medium-high
heat, sauté the celery and onion in the butter until tender, 3 to 5
minutes. Transfer to a large bowl and mix in the remaining ingredients, except the paprika; place the mixture in a 7" × 11" baking
dish that has been coated with nonstick vegetable spray. Sprinkle
the top with paprika. Bake for 45 to 55 minutes or until firm and
light golden.

True-Blue Potato Salad

about 6 servings

Blue cheese potato salad?! Sure! With always-good Wisconsin dairy products, you could make almost anything into a dairy dish. And this one is both rich and mellow . . . a real picnic hero-maker!

1½ to 2 pounds potatoes (2 to 3 large potatoes), cooked and cut into ¾-inch cubes to yield 4 cups

1 cup diced celery

½ cup sliced scallions

1¼ cups sour cream

2 tablespoons minced fresh parsley

2 tablespoons white wine vinegar

½ teaspoon celery seed

½ teaspoon salt

¼ teaspoon pepper

¾ cup (3 ounces) crumbled blue cheese

In a large bowl, combine the potato cubes, celery, and scallions; set aside. In a medium-sized bowl, combine the sour cream, parsley, vinegar, celery seed, salt, and pepper; mix well. Stir in the blue cheese. Pour over the potato mixture and toss lightly. Chill and serve.

Whipped Potato Salad

about 8 servings

*Our Midwestern potato salads are made to please, 'cause they're
so versatile. See how they please your eaters this way!*

8 medium-sized potatoes, peeled and cut into chunks	1 teaspoon prepared mustard
¼ cup pickle relish	¼ teaspoon salt
¼ cup milk	¼ teaspoon pepper
2 tablespoons butter	6 hard-boiled eggs, coarsely chopped
2 tablespoons mayonnaise	1 cup frozen peas, thawed (or chopped green bell pepper)

Place the potatoes in a large pot, add enough salted water to cover, and bring to a boil. Reduce heat to medium and simmer for 25 to 30 minutes, or until the potatoes are tender. Drain and reserve the cooking water. Mash the potatoes, then add the pickle relish, milk, butter, mayonnaise, mustard, salt, and pepper. Whip well, adding the reserved cooking water as needed to achieve the desired consistency. Stir in the eggs and peas. Serve warm or chilled.

NOTE: If you'd prefer, go ahead and start with instant mashed potatoes instead of fresh.

Linguine with Fresh Tomatoes

4 to 6 servings

*Since now we can have great tomatoes year-round, we can always
enjoy their fresh flavor this way. (And remember . . . never
store your fresh tomatoes in the refrigerator—the cold
ruins their taste and texture. Keep them right on
the counter so they'll be sweeter and juicier.)*

½ cup plus 1 tablespoon olive oil, divided
2 teaspoons salt, divided
1 pound linguine
1 tablespoon dried basil
3 garlic cloves, peeled and minced
½ teaspoon black pepper

4 large ripe tomatoes, diced
1 pound (4 cups) shredded mozzarella cheese
½ cup chicken stock
½ of a red bell pepper, diced
2 tablespoons grated Parmesan cheese (optional)

Place 1 tablespoon olive oil and 1½ teaspoons salt in a large pot of boiling water; add the linguine and cook until tender but still firm, 8 to 10 minutes. Drain, rinse with warm water, and drain again; set aside. Meanwhile, in a small saucepan, combine the basil, garlic, black pepper, the remaining ½ cup olive oil, and ½ teaspoon salt. Warm over a low heat, stirring occasionally. In a large bowl, combine the tomatoes, mozzarella, and heated oil mixture. Add the warm linguine and toss with the tomato mixture, chicken stock, red pepper, and Parmesan cheese, if desired. Serve immediately.

Little Italy Macaroni and Cheese

6 servings

Here's a version of our old favorite that you'll come back to again and again! And look how simple!

1 jar (32 ounces) meatless spaghetti sauce	1 teaspoon Italian seasoning
⅔ cup water	2 cups (8 ounces) uncooked elbow macaroni
1 container (15 ounces) ricotta cheese	1 package (8 ounces) shredded mozzarella cheese, divided
3 eggs, lightly beaten	

Preheat the oven to 350°F. In a large bowl, mix together all the ingredients except 1 cup of the mozzarella cheese. Pour the mixture into a 9" × 13" baking dish that has been coated with nonstick vegetable spray; cover with aluminum foil and bake for 45 minutes. Remove the foil, sprinkle with the remaining mozzarella cheese, and bake for an additional 15 minutes, or until the cheese is bubbly. Remove from the oven and let stand for 10 minutes before serving.

Louisiana-Style Linguine

3 to 4 servings

*Here's a pasta dish full of classic Louisiana flavor.
It's sure to satisfy everyone's appetite!*

12 ounces linguine or your favorite long pasta shape

½ cup (2 ounces) diced cooked lean ham or turkey ham

1 garlic clove, minced

½ cup chopped onion

2 tablespoons dry white wine

1 can (14½ ounces) stewed tomatoes, undrained

¼ cup chopped green bell pepper

¼ cup chopped red bell pepper

½ cup minced celery

Hot pepper sauce to taste

1 can (4.25 ounces) tiny shrimp

In a large pot of boiling salted water, cook the pasta to desired doneness; drain and place in a large serving bowl. Meanwhile, coat a large nonstick skillet with nonstick vegetable spray. Add the ham and garlic and brown over medium-high heat. Stir in the onion and wine. Cook, stirring, for 1 minute, then add the remaining ingredients and cook until heated through. Spoon over the pasta and serve.

Mulberry Street Pasta with Vegetables

4 side-dish servings (5 cups)

Take a shortcut to Little Italy and, before you know it, this
will be a regular at your house, too!

1½ cups (about ½ of a 16-ounce package) frozen mixed vegetables containing broccoli, thawed

1 garlic clove, minced

2 tablespoons butter

1 can (10¾ ounces) condensed broccoli cheese soup

1 cup milk

¼ cup grated Parmesan cheese

½ teaspoon salt

½ teaspoon Italian seasoning

3 cups hot cooked fettuccine (about 8 ounces uncooked)

In a large skillet over medium heat, cook the thawed vegetables and garlic in the butter for 5 to 8 minutes, or until tender-crisp, stirring often. Stir in the soup, milk, cheese, salt, and Italian seasoning. Bring to a boil; reduce heat to low and cook for 5 minutes, stirring occasionally. Pour the mixture over the hot fettuccine and toss to coat.

Pasta and White Bean Salad

4 servings

*Perk up your next picnic or special lunch with this
easy, tasty change of pace!*

1   pound ziti, bow ties or other
    medium pasta shape
1   can (15½ ounces) white
    beans, rinsed and drained
¼   cup sliced pimiento-stuffed
    green olives
2   tablespoons chopped fresh
    basil
2   garlic cloves, minced

¼   cup bottled Italian dressing
2   tablespoons grated Parmesan
    cheese
½   cup mayonnaise
4   hard-boiled eggs, chopped
¼   teaspoon salt

In a large pot of boiling water, cook the pasta to desired doneness; drain, rinse under cold water, and drain again. In a large bowl,
mix together all the remaining ingredients; add the pasta and toss
thoroughly.

NOTE: For a Midwestern flavor, add 2 teaspoons sweet green pickle
relish.

Ranch Macaroni and Cheese

about 6 servings

*It doesn't matter whether you're at home "on the range" or
in the city—this is a dish everyone goes for.*

2 cups elbow macaroni
¼ cup chopped onion (optional)
3 tablespoons butter
2 tablespoons all-purpose flour
½ teaspoon salt
⅛ teaspoon pepper

½ teaspoon mustard powder
2 cups milk
¼ cup ranch salad dressing
2 cups (8 ounces) shredded
   mild Cheddar cheese, divided

Preheat the oven to 350°F. In a large pot of boiling water, cook the macaroni to desired doneness; drain, transfer to a large bowl, and set aside. Meanwhile, in a medium-sized saucepan over medium heat, sauté the onion, if desired, in the butter for about 5 minutes, or until tender. Stir in the flour, salt, pepper, and mustard powder. Gradually add the milk and cook, stirring occasionally, until thickened. Remove from heat. Add the ranch dressing and 1½ cups of the Cheddar cheese; stir until the cheese melts. Combine the cheese sauce with the cooked macaroni. Place in a 1½-quart casserole that has been coated with nonstick vegetable spray and top with the remaining ½ cup Cheddar cheese. Bake for about 30 minutes or until bubbly and cheese is golden brown.

San Francisco Pasta with Chicken

about 4 servings

*Here's a great example of San Francisco-style
cooking that you're sure to love . . . pasta, chicken, and
Asian flavors all in one!*

½ pound (8 ounces) spiral-shaped pasta

1 pound chicken breasts, skinned, boned, and cut into bite-sized pieces

1 teaspoon vegetable oil

⅛ teaspoon cayenne pepper

1 bunch scallions, cut diagonally into 1-inch slices

1 cup pineapple juice

1 tablespoon honey

1½ teaspoons ground ginger or 1 tablespoon grated fresh ginger

1 tablespoon soy sauce

¼ teaspoon sesame oil

1 tablespoon cornstarch

1 tablespoon fresh lemon juice

1 tablespoon butter

2 teaspoons hoisin sauce

¼ teaspoon salt

Preheat the oven to 350°F. In a large pot of boiling water, cook the pasta to desired doneness; drain. Place the pasta in a large bowl; keep warm and set aside. Place the chicken in an 8-inch-square baking pan, brush with oil, and sprinkle with the cayenne pepper, then the scallions. Bake for 10 to 15 minutes, or until the chicken is done. Set aside to cool. Meanwhile, in a small saucepan, combine the pineapple juice, honey, ginger, soy sauce, sesame oil, and cornstarch. Bring to a boil, then whisk in the lemon juice and butter; mix well and remove from heat. Add the chicken to the pasta, then add the pineapple juice mixture, hoisin sauce, and salt; toss to mix thoroughly. Serve immediately.

Second Street Chicken and Pasta

4 to 6 servings

When I was growing up in Troy, New York, all the neighborhood kids would make a beeline to our kitchen door when they knew my mom was making this for us.

2	tablespoons olive oil	1	teaspoon dried basil
2	pounds chicken breasts, skinned, boned, and cut into chunks	1	teaspoon dried oregano
		¼	teaspoon crushed red pepper
½	cup chopped onion	1	package (16 ounces) thin spaghetti, uncooked
1	garlic clove, minced		Grated Parmesan cheese for sprinkling
1	jar (25 to 29 ounces) spaghetti sauce		
2	tablespoons chopped fresh parsley		

In a large skillet, heat the oil over medium-high heat. Add the chicken, onion, and garlic; cook until the chicken and onion are tender, 5 to 7 minutes, stirring occasionally. Stir in the spaghetti sauce, parsley, basil, oregano, and crushed red pepper. Reduce the heat and simmer, covered, stirring frequently, for about 10 minutes, or until the chicken is cooked and no pink remains. Meanwhile, in a large pot of boiling salted water, cook the pasta to desired doneness; drain. Serve the sauce over the hot pasta. Sprinkle with Parmesan cheese.

NOTE: When I was growing up, we used whichever chicken parts we happened to have. And back then we didn't use cheese on top, but it sure does make it sensational!

Southwest Macaroni Salad

6 servings

*Pasta salad and authentic Southwestern flavors are popular
everywhere, so you've got a sure winner here.*

1	pound mostaccioli, ziti, or other medium pasta shape	3	garlic cloves, minced
1	can (16 ounces) black beans, rinsed and drained	2	tablespoons vegetable oil
		½	cup mayonnaise
1	package (10 ounces) frozen corn, thawed	¼	cup red wine vinegar
		1	tablespoon chopped fresh parsley
2	cups (about 1 pint) cherry tomatoes, halved	½	teaspoon salt
½	cup finely diced red onion	¼	teaspoon pepper

In a large pot of boiling salted water, cook the pasta to desired
doneness; drain, rinse under cold water, and drain again. In a large
bowl, mix together all the remaining ingredients; stir in the pasta.
Cover and chill for about 1 hour.

Southwest Steak and Pasta

6 to 8 servings

An exciting, spicy way to enjoy steak and peppers
in the Old Southwest tradition!

½ pound (8 ounces) linguine or other long pasta shape

2 tablespoons vegetable oil

1 medium-sized onion, finely chopped (about 1½ cups)

½ of a red bell pepper, cut into thin strips

½ of a green bell pepper, cut into thin strips

1 pound top round steak, thinly sliced, then cut into thin strips

1 jar (25 to 29 ounces) spaghetti sauce

1 teaspoon ground cumin

1 teaspoon salt

¼ teaspoon black pepper

1 cup (4 ounces) shredded Monterey Jack cheese

In a large pot of boiling salted water, cook the pasta until tender; drain and set aside. Meanwhile, in a large skillet, heat the vegetable oil until hot; sauté the onion and peppers over medium heat until soft, about 5 minutes. Add the beef and sauté, stirring constantly, until brown. Remove from the heat and transfer to a 9" × 13" baking dish. Add the pasta and mix. Preheat the oven to 400°F. In a medium-sized saucepan, heat the spaghetti sauce, cumin, salt, and black pepper. Mix the sauce with the pasta, beef, and vegetables; top with the cheese and place in the oven for 1 to 2 minutes, or just until the cheese melts. Serve immediately.

Spinach Manicotti

7 servings

Packed with veggies and full of flavor. . .

14 manicotti shells

½ cup diced onion

2 garlic cloves, minced

1 cup diced fresh mushrooms (about 2 to 3 ounces)

1 egg

1 cup (4 ounces) shredded mozzarella cheese

3 cups (2 15-ounce containers) ricotta cheese

1 package (10 ounces) frozen spinach, thawed and drained well

1 teaspoon dried basil

1 teaspoon dried oregano

2 teaspoons fresh dill or 1 teaspoon dried dillweed

¾ teaspoon salt

½ teaspoon pepper

2 cups prepared spaghetti sauce

¼ cup grated Parmesan cheese

In a large pot of boiling salted water, cook the pasta to desired doneness; drain, rinse under cold water, and drain again. Place the shells in a large baking dish. Preheat the oven to 400°F. In a small saucepan that has been coated with nonstick vegetable spray, heat the onion and garlic over medium heat until soft. Add the mushrooms and sauté until brown. Meanwhile, in a large bowl, combine the egg, mozzarella and ricotta cheeses, spinach, basil, oregano, dill, salt, and pepper. Add the onion mixture and mix well. Spoon the mixture into the manicotti shells, top with the spaghetti sauce, and sprinkle with Parmesan cheese. Cover with foil and bake for 30 minutes, or until bubbly. Uncover and bake until the cheese is lightly browned, about 4 to 5 minutes more.

NOTE: An easy, efficient way to fill the pasta is to carefully place the cheese mixture in a large resealable plastic storage bag with a corner snipped off; then squeeze the filling into the pasta, using the storage bag like a pastry bag.

Summer Twist Salad

about 6 servings

How 'bout trying this new "twist" with an old favorite?
The twists are so much fun!

2 cups twist pasta or any medium pasta shape
1 cup (4 ounces) sliced fresh mushrooms
1 medium-sized zucchini, sliced
1 cup (4 ounces) Cheddar cheese cubes
½ cup pitted black olives, drained
¾ cup mayonnaise
¼ cup chili sauce
2 hard-boiled eggs, finely chopped
¼ cup chopped green bell pepper
½ teaspoon dried dillweed
¼ teaspoon salt
¼ teaspoon black pepper

In a large pot of boiling salted water, cook the pasta to desired doneness; drain and rinse under cold water. Drain again and place in a large bowl. Add the mushrooms, zucchini, Cheddar cheese, and olives. Toss to mix well. In a medium-sized bowl, mix together the remaining ingredients. Add the mayonnaise mixture to the pasta and toss to coat. Cover and chill.

NOTE: Serve on individual salad plates over lettuce leaves.

Sun-Dried Tomato Pasta

about 8 servings

Is heaven a U.S. region? It must be, 'cause this salad is divine.

¾ cup balsamic vinegar
1 package (3 ounces) sun-dried tomatoes (not in oil)
2 garlic cloves, peeled
1 small onion, peeled
1 tablespoon olive oil
1 tablespoon sugar
1 teaspoon Italian seasoning

1 pound rotini or shell pasta
1 small cucumber, chopped
1 small green bell pepper, chopped
1 small zucchini, chopped
2 cups (about 5 ounces) sliced mushrooms
½ cup grated Parmesan cheese

In a small saucepan, heat the vinegar just to boiling. Add the sun-dried tomatoes and remove from the heat; cover and set aside, allowing to soak for 10 minutes. Meanwhile, in a blender or food processor, combine the garlic, onion, olive oil, sugar, and Italian seasoning. Drain the sun-dried tomatoes, discarding the vinegar, and add to the blender; blend until all the ingredients are chopped and mixed well. In a large pot of boiling salted water, cook the pasta to desired doneness; drain, rinse under cold water, and drain again. Place in a large bowl, then toss with the sun-dried tomato mixture and the remaining ingredients. Cover and chill for 1 to 2 hours.

Tex-Mex Pasta Salad

15 to 18 servings

*Avocados, peppers, and beans . . . that's a fresh Southwestern combo!
And if you don't have avocados—throw in
an extra can of beans.*

1 box (16 ounces) twist pasta	2 garlic cloves, minced
1 red or green bell pepper, chopped	¾ teaspoon ground cumin
1 can (16 ounces) black beans or kidney beans, drained	1 small avocado, peeled and chopped
½ cup sliced black olives	1 tablespoon fresh lemon or lime juice
1 jar (16 ounces) salsa	⅓ cup grated Parmesan cheese
½ cup sour cream	

In a large pot of boiling salted water, cook the pasta to desired doneness; drain, rinse under cold water, drain again, and place in a large bowl. Add the pepper, beans, and olives. In a medium-sized bowl, combine the salsa, sour cream, garlic, and cumin; add to the pasta mixture. In a small bowl, toss the avocado with the lemon juice, then gently blend with the pasta mixture. Sprinkle with the Parmesan cheese and serve.

Bean Salad

6 to 8 servings

*Beans are "in" all over the country—and beans
are easy (especially when you use canned)!*

1 can (14 to 16 ounces) great
Northern or white kidney
beans, undrained

1 can (14 to 16 ounces)
garbanzo beans (chick peas),
undrained

⅓ cup olive oil

¼ cup lemon juice

3 scallions, chopped

1 tablespoon chopped red bell
pepper

½ teaspoon dried basil

¾ teaspoon salt

¼ teaspoon black pepper

Place the beans in a medium-sized saucepan; bring to a boil,
then drain. Mix in the remaining ingredients. Let cool, then transfer
to a storage container and store, covered, in the refrigerator. Serve
chilled.

Carrot Bake

6 to 9 servings

*In California they serve lots of vegetable dishes, and this
is one of my favorites 'cause it's an exciting new one!*

1   pound fresh or frozen carrots,
    cooked and mashed

6   tablespoons (¾ stick) butter,
    softened

4   eggs

1   cup cracker meal

¾   cup milk

¾   cup shredded Cheddar
    cheese

1   tablespoon minced onion

1   tablespoon sugar

1½ teaspoons dried dillweed

2   teaspoons seasoned salt

Preheat the oven to 350°F. Place the mashed carrots in a large
bowl; add the butter and mix well. Add the eggs, one at a time,
beating after each addition. Stir in the remaining ingredients. Pour
the mixture into a greased 1½-quart casserole dish or an 8-inch-
square baking pan, and bake for 50 to 60 minutes or until light
golden. Let cool for 10 minutes, then run a knife around the outside
of the pan. Cut into serving-sized pieces and serve.

Corn Fancy

8 servings

What a fancy way to celebrate America's Heartland!
(And it's so simple!!)

1 can (16½ ounces) cream-style corn	4 eggs, well beaten
½ cup vegetable oil	½ cup corn muffin mix (1 7½-ounce box is about 1½ cups)
½ teaspoon garlic salt	
1 jar (2 ounces) chopped pimientos, drained	1½ cups (6 ounces) shredded Cheddar cheese

Preheat the oven to 300°F. In a large bowl, combine all the ingredients except the cheese; mix well. Pour the mixture into a greased 1½-quart casserole or baking dish. Bake for 30 minutes. Sprinkle the top with the cheese, then bake for 15 minutes more or until the cheese melts.

Corn Puddings

Everybody likes corn, so here are two ways to enjoy it anytime. (The first is a bit more flavorful, but both are great!)

Autumn Corn Pudding

about 8 servings

2 cans (17 ounces each) whole-kernel corn

1 can (16½ ounces) cream-style corn

1 sleeve saltine crackers, crushed

2 drops vanilla extract

¼ cup firmly packed brown sugar

6 eggs, well beaten

Dash of pepper

Dash of ground cinnamon or nutmeg (optional)

Preheat the oven to 350°F. In a large bowl, combine all the ingredients; mix well. Place in a 2½-quart casserole dish that has been coated with nonstick vegetable spray, and bake for about 1 hour, or until golden and set.

Easy Corn Pudding

about 6 servings

1 can (17 ounces) whole-kernel corn

1 can (16½ ounces) cream-style corn

¼ cup milk

¼ cup sugar

2 eggs, beaten

2 tablespoons cornstarch

Preheat the oven to 350°F. In a large bowl, combine all the ingredients; mix well. Place in a 1½- or 2-quart casserole that has been coated with nonstick vegetable spray, and bake for about 70 minutes, or until golden and set.

Crunchy Salad

4 servings

Here's a chunky fresh salad with just the right
Salinas Valley crunch!

3 cups broccoli florets

¾ cup sliced celery, cut diagonally into ¼-inch-wide pieces

¼ cup finely chopped onion

⅓ cup grated Cheddar cheese

¼ cup mayonnaise

¼ cup sour cream

½ teaspoon seasoned salt

⅛ teaspoon pepper

In a medium-sized bowl, combine the broccoli, celery, onion, and cheese; set aside. In a small bowl, combine the remaining ingredients. Add the mayonnaise mixture to the vegetable mixture and toss. Cover and refrigerate for at least 2 hours to "marry" the flavors.

NOTE: This is great as is or you can "fancy it up" by serving it over lettuce or with sliced tomatoes. And if you want a lighter version, use a light cheese and a light mayonnaise.

Florida Glazed Carrots and Parsnips

about 4 servings

Vegetables kissed with Florida sunshine . . . sweet and mellow, too.

6 medium-sized carrots, peeled and diagonally sliced into 1-inch pieces

6 medium-sized parsnips, peeled and diagonally sliced into 1-inch pieces

¼ cup freshly squeezed orange juice (about ½ of a large orange)

¼ cup honey

2 tablespoons (¼ stick) butter

½ teaspoon freshly grated orange peel

In a medium-sized saucepan, cook the carrots in boiling salted water for 2 to 3 minutes; add the parsnips and cook for an additional 3 to 5 minutes, or until the vegetables are almost tender. Drain the water and add the remaining ingredients; reduce heat to medium and cook for 2 to 3 minutes, until the vegetables are tender and evenly glazed, tossing occasionally.

NOTE: This can be made without the parsnips if you'd prefer all carrots. Just adjust the cooking time to cook all the carrots until almost tender, then drain and continue as above.

Fresh Green Bean Salad

6 to 8 servings

*This is so delicious that the kids won't notice
how packed it is with garden freshness! No fresh
beans around? Use frozen ones.*

1 pound fresh green beans, trimmed and blanched	1 tablespoon red wine vinegar
½ of a small red onion, thinly sliced	2 tablespoons water
½ cup garbanzo beans (chick peas), rinsed and drained	2 teaspoons vegetable oil
1 cup cherry tomatoes, halved	1 teaspoon basil leaves
	¼ teaspoon mustard powder
	¼ teaspoon salt

In a large bowl, combine the green beans, onion, chick peas, and cherry tomatoes. In a medium-sized bowl, combine the remaining ingredients, then pour over the vegetables and toss. Chill.

NOTE: There's no need to trim and blanch frozen green beans. If using them, just thaw, drain well, and combine with the onion slices, garbanzo beans, and cherry tomatoes as directed.

Homestyle Cabbage

6 to 8 servings

Delight the family with a wholesome New England–style dish they'll love.

1 medium-sized cabbage, cut into 6 wedges, core removed

1 medium-sized onion, thinly sliced

1 green bell pepper, thinly sliced into rings

1 tablespoon sugar

2 tablespoons (¼ stick) butter

1 can (28 ounces) whole tomatoes, drained, broken up

⅛ teaspoon salt

⅛ teaspoon black pepper

1 cup (4 ounces) shredded Cheddar cheese

Preheat the oven to 350°F. Place the cabbage wedges in a large pot; add about 1 inch of lightly salted water, cover, and boil for 10 minutes. Meanwhile, in a medium-sized saucepan over medium heat, cook the onion, green pepper, and sugar in the butter until the vegetables are tender, stirring constantly. Stir in the tomatoes, salt, and black pepper. Drain the cabbage well, then carefully place the wedges in a greased 9" × 13" baking pan. Pour the vegetable mixture over the cabbage. Sprinkle the cheese over the vegetables and bake for 20 to 30 minutes or until heated through.

Marinated Asparagus

3 to 4 servings

This recipe (that I first tried with some of that great Michigan asparagus) is now being done at buffets all around the country. Now you can do it, too.

1 pound asparagus, lightly cooked (still crunchy), drained

MARINADE

¼ cup vegetable oil

2 tablespoons white vinegar

1 jar (2 ounces) chopped pimientos, drained (2 tablespoons)

½ teaspoon chopped garlic

1 tablespoon dried parsley flakes

1 teaspoon salt

½ teaspoon pepper

½ teaspoon mustard powder

Place the cooked asparagus in a shallow serving dish. Combine the marinade ingredients in a jar or other leakproof container; cover tightly and shake well. Pour over the asparagus, cover, and chill for at least 4 hours before serving.

NOTE: You can enjoy this even after asparagus season by using canned or frozen asparagus (and you don't even have to cook those first). And you can make it even easier by using ½ cup of a bottled Italian dressing instead of making this marinade from scratch.

Mock Crabmeat Salad

about 4 servings

They'll think they're getting a seacoast original—
they'll never guess it's parsnips . . . amazing!

2 cups shredded raw parsnips
(about 1½ pounds)

8 to 9 green or black olives,
chopped

1 jar (2 ounces) chopped
pimientos, drained

1 cup diced celery

1 small onion, grated or minced

¼ teaspoon salt

¼ teaspoon pepper

About ½ cup Thousand Island
dressing or mayonnaise to
moisten

Combine all the ingredients in a medium-sized bowl. Cover, chill, and serve.

NOTE: Use more or less dressing, depending on your individual preference. Serve over lettuce.

Pepper Patch Salad

about 4 servings

Every season is pepper season, so serve this extra-special Southwestern-style salad at any meal, anytime, anyplace.
(Great for picnics, too!)

1 medium-sized onion, thinly sliced

2 garlic cloves, minced

1 small yellow, orange, or red bell pepper, cut into short, thin strips

1 small green bell pepper, cut into short, thin strips

¼ cup regular or reduced-calorie bottled Italian dressing

½ cup picante sauce

1 large fresh tomato, seeded and cut into ½-inch pieces

2 tablespoons coarsely chopped fresh cilantro (optional)

In a large skillet, sauté the onion, garlic, and peppers in the dressing over medium heat for 3 to 4 minutes. Reduce the heat to low, add the picante sauce and cook, uncovered, for 5 minutes more, stirring occasionally. Remove from the heat and stir in the tomato and cilantro. Chill before serving.

Spinach Soufflé

4 to 6 servings

*There's something elegant about soufflé. And there's
something great about this one: It's easy!*

½ cup mayonnaise
¼ cup all-purpose flour
2 tablespoons grated onion
¼ teaspoon garlic powder
¾ teaspoon salt
½ teaspoon pepper
¼ teaspoon ground nutmeg

1 cup milk
1 package (10 ounces) frozen chopped spinach, thawed and drained well
4 eggs, separated
¼ teaspoon cream of tartar

Preheat the oven to 400°F. In a medium-sized saucepan, stir together the mayonnaise, flour, onion, garlic powder, salt, pepper, and nutmeg. Cook over medium heat for 1 minute, stirring constantly; gradually add the milk, stirring until smooth; continue cooking until thick, 3 to 4 minutes, stirring constantly. *Do not boil.* Remove from heat, beat in the spinach, then the egg yolks; set aside. In a small bowl, beat the egg whites and cream of tartar with an electric mixer on high speed until stiff peaks form; fold into the spinach mixture (do not overmix). Spoon the mixture into a greased 2-quart soufflé or casserole dish; place on the lowest rack of the oven and immediately reduce the temperature to 375°F. Bake for at least 40 minutes, or until the top is puffed and has a golden-brown crust. Serve immediately.

Spring Casserole

about 8 servings

*In the sweet onion–growing areas, folks rave about how sweet
their onions are. When you put this on the table,
folks will rave about how sweet **you** are!*

7½ to 8 cups chopped sweet
    onions (4 to 5 large onions)
¼ cup (½ stick) butter
5   cups salted water

½ cup uncooked rice
¾ cup grated Swiss cheese
⅔ cup half-and-half

Preheat the oven to 300°F. In a large skillet over medium heat, sauté the onions in the butter until soft and light golden. Place in a large bowl and set aside. Meanwhile, bring the water to a boil in a large saucepan; add the rice and cook for 5 minutes, then drain. Add the rice to the onions and mix well. Mix in the cheese and half-and-half. Pour into a greased 2-quart casserole dish and bake, covered, for 1 hour.

NOTE: This is a great side dish that'll go with everything from a barbecue to a fancy dinner. Give it your own special touch . . . try fresh parsley, basil, dill, or any of your favorite seasonings.

Succotash

4 to 6 servings

A traditional favorite in the Northeast!!

½ cup chopped scallions

1 medium-sized red bell pepper, chopped

¼ cup (½ stick) butter

1 bag (20 ounces) frozen butternut squash cubes, thawed

1 package (10 ounces) frozen baby lima beans, thawed

1 package (10 ounces) frozen corn kernels, thawed

½ cup water

¾ teaspoon salt

½ teaspoon black pepper

½ teaspoon onion powder

In a large skillet over medium heat, sauté the scallions and red pepper in the butter until soft, about 5 minutes. Cover the skillet, reduce heat to low, and cook for about 10 minutes. Add the squash, lima beans, corn, and water, stirring to blend. Cover and cook until the vegetables are tender and the liquid is absorbed, 15 to 20 minutes. Season with the salt, pepper, and onion powder, and serve.

Summer Tomatoes and Onions

3 to 4 servings

When your garden is overflowing with luscious, ripe tomatoes, here's a delicious idea that'll become one of your regulars.

MARINADE

¼ cup vegetable or olive oil

1 tablespoon wine vinegar

½ teaspoon dried basil

½ teaspoon dried oregano

½ teaspoon sugar

¼ teaspoon salt

¼ teaspoon coarse ground black pepper

⅛ teaspoon mustard powder

½ teaspoon garlic powder

2 large, ripe tomatoes at room temperature

1 small sweet onion, thinly sliced

2 tablespoons chopped fresh parsley

In a medium-sized bowl, combine the marinade ingredients; mix well and set aside. Cut the tomatoes into ¼-inch-thick slices. In a shallow serving dish, arrange half of the tomato slices in a single layer; sprinkle half of the onion slices and parsley over the top and drizzle with half of the marinade. Repeat. Cover and let stand at room temperature for 1 hour. Serve.

ThanKevin Coleslaw

about 8 servings

Don't be shocked when you read this whip-up-and-serve idea.
There'll be a lot of thanks to you
for serving this at your table.

1 cup heavy cream
½ cup sugar
⅓ cup white vinegar

1 medium-sized head of
  cabbage, shredded (about
  12 cups)
1 carrot, shredded

In a medium-sized bowl, whip the heavy cream until fluffy. Mix in the sugar and vinegar. Place the cabbage in a large bowl; pour the cream mixture over it, add the shredded carrot, and mix well. Serve immediately or cover and chill until ready to serve.

Vegetable Pita Pizzas

4 servings

*Tell your family it's like a quick trip to Las Vegas
(well, that's where I first enjoyed these).*

1	teaspoon olive oil	¼	teaspoon dried thyme leaves
1	small onion, cut into thin wedges	¼	teaspoon crushed red pepper
2	garlic cloves, minced	¼	teaspoon salt (optional)
2	small green bell peppers, cut into thin strips about 1 inch long	4	6-inch pita breads
		4	tomatoes, thinly sliced
¼	cup chicken broth	1½	cups (6 ounces) shredded mozzarella cheese
1	teaspoon dried basil		

Preheat the broiler. Heat the oil in a large skillet over medium heat. Cook the onion and garlic for 2 minutes, stirring occasionally. Add the pepper strips, broth, basil, thyme, crushed red pepper, and salt; cook for 5 minutes or until the vegetables are tender, stirring occasionally. Place the pitas on a broiler pan or cookie sheet. Layer the tomato slices evenly over the pitas, then top with the warm vegetable mixture. Sprinkle the mozzarella cheese evenly over the vegetables, then broil 5 to 6 inches from the heat source for 1 minute or just until the cheese is melted.

Breads and Muffins

"Bapple" Bread

1 loaf

Two great flavors, one great bread.
(And no oil!)

4 ripe bananas	1 tablespoon baking powder
1 cup sugar	1 teaspoon salt
½ cup applesauce	1 teaspoon vanilla extract
2 eggs	2 cups all-purpose flour
1 teaspoon baking soda	

Preheat the oven to 350°F. Place the bananas in a large bowl and mash with an electric mixer. Stir in the sugar and let stand for 15 minutes. Add the applesauce and eggs and beat well. Add the remaining ingredients and mix thoroughly. Pour into a 9" × 5" loaf pan that has been coated with nonstick vegetable spray. Bake for 45 minutes, or until a wooden toothpick inserted in the center comes out clean. Remove from the oven and let stand for 10 minutes before removing from the pan. Cool on a wire rack.

Cayenne Corn Bread

6 to 9 servings

*Corn bread has always been a big hit in the Southwest—
and in the rest of the country now, too!*

2 eggs

1 can (8¾ ounces) cream-style corn

1 cup sour cream

1 cup (4 ounces) shredded Cheddar cheese

1 cup yellow cornmeal

2 tablespoons sugar

1 teaspoon baking soda

½ teaspoon cayenne pepper

3 tablespoons butter, divided

Preheat the oven to 400°F. In a medium-sized bowl, lightly beat the eggs. Add the remaining ingredients, except the butter; mix well. Melt 1 tablespoon of the butter and stir it into the batter. Place the remaining 2 tablespoons of butter in a large cast-iron skillet or a 9-inch square baking pan and place in the oven until the butter melts. Immediately pour the batter into the pan. Bake for 25 minutes or until golden brown and the center is firm.

Chunky Apple Bran Muffins

10 muffins

*From the orchards of New York State come these bran muffins
that are deliciously good for us.*

2 egg whites
1 cup chunky applesauce
½ teaspoon ground cinnamon

1 teaspoon vanilla extract
1 box (7 ounces) bran muffin
    mix (plain or with dates)

Preheat the oven to 400°F. In a large bowl, combine all the ingredients. Spoon the mixture evenly into 10 lined muffin tins and bake for 15 to 20 minutes or until the muffins are golden brown.

Easy Pumpkin Bread

1 loaf

As you smell this wonderful bread baking, just imagine the Pennsylvania growing fields bursting with ready-to-pick, bright orange pumpkins.

1½ cups sugar	2 eggs
1¼ cups all-purpose flour	1 teaspoon baking soda
1 cup canned solid-pack pumpkin	¼ teaspoon ground allspice
½ cup vegetable oil	½ teaspoon ground cinnamon
½ cup raisins	½ teaspoon ground nutmeg
½ cup chopped walnuts	¼ teaspoon baking powder
⅓ cup water	

Preheat the oven to 350°F. In a large bowl, combine all the ingredients; mix well and pour into a 9" × 5" loaf pan that has been coated with nonstick vegetable spray. Bake for about 1¼ hours or until a wooden toothpick inserted in the center comes out clean. Let cool for 10 minutes before slicing.

Golden Herb Bread

1 loaf

This will fill your kitchen with home-baked good smells, and
thrill your taste buds with homemade good flavors . . .
with so little effort!

1 1-pound loaf frozen bread
   dough
2 tablespoons butter, melted
¼ teaspoon onion powder

1½ teaspoons Italian seasoning
1   egg, beaten

Thaw the bread dough according to the package directions. In a medium-sized bowl, combine the remaining ingredients. Cut the dough into 1-inch cubes, dip the dough pieces into the butter mixture, then layer them in a greased 9" × 5" loaf pan. Cover loosely with buttered plastic wrap, buttered side down, and let rise until doubled in size (about 45 minutes to 1 hour). Meanwhile, preheat the oven to 375°F., then bake the bread for 25 minutes or until golden brown on top. Remove from the oven and let sit for 10 minutes before removing from pan.

NOTE: Frozen bread dough typically comes 3 to a pack. Why not make all 3 and get 3 times the OOH it's so GOOD!!™

Holiday ''Quickie'' Garlic Bread

4 to 6 servings

The name says it—it's quick and easy to make
(and it disappears in a flash)!

1 cup (4 ounces) shredded
  Cheddar cheese
1 cup grated Parmesan cheese
1 cup mayonnaise

½ teaspoon garlic powder
1 loaf Italian or French bread,
  split lengthwise

Preheat the broiler. In a large bowl, combine the cheeses, mayonnaise, and garlic powder. Place the bread on a cookie sheet, spread the cheese mixture over, and broil for a few minutes, until the cheese is golden brown and bubbly.

NOTE: This is great served with fruit or wine. For some variety, you might try sprinkling it with dried basil, rosemary, or chili powder. You can even place sliced tomatoes on the uncooked garlic bread, drizzle it with some prepared pesto sauce, sprinkle it with cheese, and broil as above.

New Garlic Bread

about 8 servings

Yet another delicious treat from those clever California cooks!

1 1-pound loaf French or Italian bread

3 tablespoons olive oil

1 medium-sized onion, chopped

2 garlic cloves, minced

1 package (9 ounces) frozen chopped spinach, thawed and well drained

1 tablespoon grated Parmesan cheese

1 teaspoon dried Italian seasoning

½ teaspoon fennel seed, crushed

1 large tomato, seeded and chopped

6 ounces (1½ cups) shredded mozzarella cheese

1 tablespoon dried basil

Fresh chopped parsley for garnish (optional)

Preheat the oven to 400°F. Cut the bread in half lengthwise and place, cut side up, on a foil-lined cookie sheet. In a medium-sized skillet, heat the oil over medium-high heat until hot. Add the onion and garlic; cook and stir until tender, about 4 to 5 minutes. Add the spinach and heat until warm, about 1 minute. Remove from heat and stir in the Parmesan cheese, Italian seasoning and fennel seed; mix well. Spread the spinach mixture evenly over the bread halves. Sprinkle with the tomato, mozzarella cheese, and basil. Bake for 8 to 10 minutes, or until the cheese is melted and the edges of the bread are golden brown. Garnish with the parsley, if desired, then cut into slices and serve.

One-Pan Banana Bread

1 loaf

Direct from Hawaii, a yummy banana-nut bread made in just one pan!

⅓ cup vegetable oil	3 eggs
1½ cups mashed ripe bananas (about 4 medium-sized bananas)	2⅓ cups biscuit baking mix
	1 cup sugar
½ teaspoon vanilla extract	½ cup chopped walnuts

Preheat the oven to 350°F. Generously grease the bottom of a 9" × 5" loaf pan. Place all the ingredients in the pan and stir with a fork until moistened; beat vigorously for 1 minute. Bake for 55 to 65 minutes or until a wooden toothpick inserted in the center comes out clean. Cool for 5 minutes. Run a knife or metal spatula around the sides of the loaf, pressing gently to loosen; remove the loaf from the pan. Cool slightly before slicing.

Peanut Muffins

1 dozen

If you're thinking of "Carolina in the Morning,"
try whipping up these muffins. They're a snap!

1½ cups all-purpose flour
1 tablespoon baking powder
¼ teaspoon salt
¼ cup sugar
2 eggs, beaten

½ cup milk
½ cup (1 stick) butter, melted
¾ cup unsalted dry roasted peanuts, chopped

Preheat the oven to 400°F. In a large bowl, combine the flour, baking powder, salt, and sugar; make a well in the center of the mixture. In a medium-sized bowl, combine the eggs, milk, and butter; pour into the well and stir just until moistened. Gently stir in the peanuts. Spoon the mixture into greased muffin tins, filling three-fourths full. Bake for about 15 minutes, or until a wooden toothpick inserted in the center comes out clean. Let cool slightly, then remove to a rack to continue cooling. Serve warm or cold.

Popovers

6 popovers

This traditional American favorite lives on!
There's something about warm popovers on a lazy
Sunday morning . . . pssst, pass the jam!

2 *cold* eggs
1 cup cold milk
1 tablespoon butter, melted

1 cup all-purpose flour
½ teaspoon salt

Preheat the oven to 425°F. Grease 6 custard cups or muffin tins. In a large bowl, combine all the ingredients and beat with a wooden spoon until smooth. Immediately pour the batter into the prepared cups or tins, filling halfway. Bake for about 35 minutes or until golden brown and puffy. Cool slightly before removing from custard cups.

NOTE: These will "pop" up better if you don't open the oven until near the end of the suggested cooking time. Serve plain, with butter, or with your favorite jam or jelly.

Poppy Seed Bread

1 loaf

Poppy seed breads are a Pennsylvania Dutch specialty, but this one's a special easy treat from Georgia.

1 can (8 ounces) crushed pineapple in unsweetened juice, drained and juice reserved

¼ cup freshly squeezed orange juice

Grated peel of 1 orange

⅓ cup milk

2 eggs

⅓ cup firmly packed light brown sugar

2 tablespoons vegetable oil

2 tablespoons poppy seed

2 cups all-purpose flour

2 teaspoons baking powder

½ teaspoon salt

Preheat the oven to 350°F. In a large bowl, combine ¼ cup of the reserved pineapple juice (discard the remaining juice or set aside for another use), the pineapple, orange juice, grated orange peel, milk, eggs, brown sugar, oil, and poppy seed. In another large bowl, combine the flour, baking powder, and salt. Add the pineapple mixture to the flour mixture, folding the batter just enough to moisten all ingredients. Do not overmix. Pour into a greased 9" × 5" loaf pan and bake for 45 to 50 minutes, or until a wooden toothpick inserted in the center comes out clean. Cool for 10 minutes, then turn out onto a rack and cool completely before slicing.

Sour Cream Corn Bread

about 9 servings

Here's some home-baked goodness that'll satisfy the heartiest of appetites. (And this one stays moister than the regular corn breads.)

1 cup all-purpose flour	1 teaspoon salt
1 cup yellow cornmeal	1 egg
4 tablespoons sugar	⅓ cup milk
2 teaspoons baking powder	¼ cup (½ stick) melted butter
½ teaspoon baking soda	1 cup (½ pint) sour cream

Preheat the oven to 400°F. In a large bowl, combine the flour, cornmeal, sugar, baking powder, baking soda, and salt. In a medium-sized bowl, beat together the egg, milk, and butter. Add the egg mixture and sour cream to the flour mixture. Stir just until blended. Pour the mixture into a greased 8-inch square baking pan. Bake for 20 to 25 minutes, or until golden and a wooden toothpick inserted in the center comes out clean.

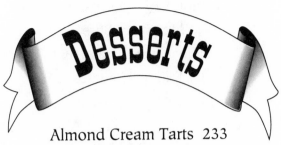

Almond Cream Tarts

6 servings

*Yes, you can make these fruit-topped cream tarts from Chicago
that look and taste just like the ones from the bakery.
(Look how easy they are!)*

4 ounces regular or light cream cheese, softened (½ of an 8-ounce package)

2 cups whole or skim milk

1 package (4-serving size) regular or sugar-free vanilla instant pudding and pie filling

½ teaspoon almond extract

1 package (6 single-serving size) graham cracker tart shells

Assorted sliced fresh fruit for garnish (like kiwifruit, berries, bananas, oranges, and peaches)

3 tablespoons regular or low-sugar apricot or peach jam, melted

Place the cream cheese, milk, pudding mix, and almond extract in a blender; cover and process at medium speed until smooth. Pour immediately into the tart shells, distributing the mixture evenly. Chill for 30 minutes, then top each tart with sliced fruit in decorative patterns. Brush the arranged fruit with the melted jam and serve, or keep topped tarts refrigerated until ready to use.

Almond Munch

about 7 cups

Try a sweet treat from bountiful California!

½ cup slivered almonds
⅓ cup butter
1   cup sugar
¼ cup light corn syrup
⅓ cup water

1   teaspoon vanilla extract
¼ teaspoon almond flavoring or extract
3   cups Crispix® cereal

In a large skillet over medium heat, cook the almonds, butter, sugar, corn syrup, and water, stirring constantly, until the mixture starts to boil. Continue to cook, stirring constantly, for 10 to 12 minutes longer, or until the almonds start to brown. Remove from heat. Carefully stir the vanilla extract and almond flavoring into the hot mixture. Add the cereal and gently stir to coat the cereal. Spread the mixture on a foil-lined 10" × 15" rimmed cookie sheet that has been coated with nonstick vegetable spray. Cool completely, then break into pieces. Store in an airtight container.

Apea Cake

6 to 8 servings

From the hills of Pennsylvania comes this cake
full of solid goodness.

2 cups all-purpose flour	⅓ cup raisins
¾ cup firmly packed light brown sugar	⅓ cup chopped walnuts
1½ teaspoons baking powder	1 egg
½ teaspoon ground cinnamon	1 teaspoon vanilla extract
½ cup (1 stick) cold butter, cut into 12 pieces	⅓ to ½ cup milk

Preheat the oven to 350°F. In a medium-sized bowl, combine the flour, brown sugar, baking powder, and cinnamon; stir to combine well. Cut in the butter, using a pastry cutter or fork, until the mixture is crumbly and forms pea-sized clumps. Stir in the raisins and walnuts. In a 1-cup glass measuring cup, beat the egg with a fork. Add the vanilla and enough milk to equal ⅔ cup total liquid. Add to the flour mixture and stir until thoroughly moistened. Transfer the batter to a 9-inch pie plate that has been coated with nonstick vegetable spray. Smooth out the top of the batter. Bake for about 30 minutes or until a wooden toothpick inserted in the center comes out clean. Let cool for at least 15 minutes before cutting. Serve warm or at room temperature.

Apple Nut Bars

about 21 bars

*Apples grow in so many states! Lucky for us, we have
lots of yummy ways to enjoy them . . . like this!*

1   cup all-purpose flour
1   cup sugar
½   teaspoon salt
¼   teaspoon baking powder
2   eggs, well beaten

¼   cup (½ stick) butter, melted
⅓   cup raisins
1   cup chopped walnuts or other nuts
1   cup finely chopped peeled apples

Preheat the oven to 350°F. In a large bowl, mix together the flour, sugar, salt, and baking powder. Add the remaining ingredients and mix well. Place the batter in a greased 9" × 13" baking pan. Bake for 40 to 50 minutes or until the edges are golden. Remove from the oven and cut into bars while still warm, but not hot.

NOTE: Before serving, you might want to roll the bars in confectioners' sugar or top them with a cream cheese frosting. Maybe serve them with whipped topping as a "dip" or serve plain as a great snack cookie.

Apple Pecan Cream Pie

8 servings

A creamy, nutty variation on our American favorite.

1 can (21 ounces) apple pie filling
2 tablespoons firmly packed brown sugar
½ teaspoon ground cinnamon
½ cup chopped pecans
1 prepared 9-inch graham cracker pie crust

½ cup cold milk
½ cup half-and-half or light cream
1 package (4-serving size) vanilla instant pudding and pie filling
1½ cups frozen whipped topping, thawed (1 8-ounce container equals 3½ cups)

In a large bowl, combine the apple pie filling, brown sugar, and cinnamon; stir in the pecans. Spread half of the mixture in the pie crust; refrigerate the remaining mixture. Place the milk and the half-and-half in a medium-sized bowl; add the pudding mix. Beat with a wire whisk until well blended, about 1 to 2 minutes. Gently stir in the whipped topping. Spoon the pudding mixture over the apple mixture in the pie crust. Freeze for at least 2 hours before serving. Remove from the freezer about 10 minutes before serving, and garnish with the reserved apple mixture and additional whipped topping, if desired.

Baked Rice Pudding

8 to 10 servings

This is a New England tradition that's easy, and easy to love! WOW!

2 cups cooked rice
3 cups milk
½ cup honey or sugar

3 eggs, slightly beaten
1 cup raisins

Preheat the oven to 350°F. In a medium-sized bowl, mix together the rice, milk, and honey. Add the eggs, then stir in the raisins. Place the mixture in a well-greased 8-inch square baking pan and bake for about 1 hour, or until golden. Cool before serving.

NOTE: Top with cream for an extra special touch.

Banana Pudding

8 to 10 servings

Even if we can't sit under a palm tree in beautiful Puerto Rico
we can dream about it as we enjoy a treat like this!

1 package (8 ounces) cream cheese, softened	24 vanilla wafers
2¼ cups milk, divided	2 cups banana slices (about 3 medium-sized bananas)
1 package (4-serving size) vanilla instant pudding and pie filling	

In a medium-sized bowl, combine the cream cheese and ½ cup of milk, mixing at medium speed with an electric mixer, until well blended. Add the remaining milk and the pudding mix; beat at low speed for 1 minute. In a 1½-quart serving bowl, layer ⅓ of the pudding mixture, half of the wafers, and half of the banana slices. Repeat layers, topping with the remaining pudding. Cover with waxed paper or plastic wrap and chill.

NOTE: Garnish with additional banana slices and wafers, if desired.

Candy Bar Pie

8 to 10 servings

This is a serious recipe for serious dessert lovers.
It's an all-time recipe request champ!

1	unbaked 9-inch pie crust	2	eggs
5	Snickers® candy bars (2.07 ounces each)	⅓	cup sour cream
½ cup sugar		⅓	cup creamy peanut butter
4	small packages (3 ounces each) cream cheese, softened	3	tablespoons heavy cream
		⅔	cup semisweet chocolate chips

Preheat the oven to 450°F. Place the pie crust in a 9-inch pie pan and bake for 5 to 7 minutes or until very light golden. Remove from the oven and let cool. Reduce the oven temperature to 325°F. Meanwhile, cut the candy bars in half lengthwise, then into ¼-inch pieces. Place the candy bar pieces over the bottom of the partially baked crust. In a small bowl, combine the sugar and cream cheese; beat until smooth. Add the eggs, one at a time, beating well after each addition. Add the sour cream and peanut butter, beating until the mixture is smooth. Pour over the candy bar pieces. Bake for 30 to 40 minutes or until the center is set. Cool completely. When the pie is cooled, heat the heavy cream in a small saucepan until very warm. Remove from the heat and stir in the chocolate chips. Stir until the chips are melted and the mixture is smooth. Spread over the top of the cooled pie. Refrigerate for 2 to 3 hours before serving. Store in the refrigerator.

Cherries Jubilee

about 8 servings

Why wait till you go to a fancy New York restaurant to enjoy this traditional favorite? With all those beautiful sour cherries grown in New York State, it's a natural there . . . and now it can be a natural in your dining room, too.

1¼ cups cold milk

1 package (4-serving size) vanilla instant pudding and pie filling

1 cup frozen whipped topping, thawed (1 8-ounce container equals 3½ cups)

2 tablespoons toasted sliced almonds, divided

1 can (20 ounces) light cherry pie filling

Pour the milk and pudding mix into a leakproof 1-quart container and shake vigorously for 45 seconds or until well blended. Gently stir in the whipped topping and 1 tablespoon of the almond slices. Alternately spoon the pudding mixture and the cherries into parfait glasses. Refrigerate until ready to serve and garnish with the remaining almonds.

Chocolate-Caramel Pecan Squares

about 48 bars

In the South, they have a knack for taking something great and making it taste even better!! Here's how they do it with their native favorite: pecans.

12 double graham crackers

2 packages (7 ounces each) chocolate-covered caramel candies (about 50 pieces)

⅓ cup heavy cream

1½ cups coarsely chopped pecans, lightly toasted*

Completely cover the bottom of a 10" × 15" rimmed cookie sheet with the graham crackers; set aside. In a heavy saucepan, heat and stir the candies and cream over low heat, until the candies melt. Spread the chocolate mixture over the graham crackers; quickly sprinkle with the nuts, gently pressing them into the chocolate. Cool for 10 to 15 minutes, then cut into bars or break into chunks like brittle. Serve immediately, or store in an airtight container until ready to serve.

NOTE: Use walnuts or peanuts . . . whatever your gang likes. And if you use peanuts, how about throwing on a few peanut butter morsels with the nuts?? You can also prepare this in the microwave by placing the candies and cream in a glass bowl, microwaving it at 30 percent power for 2 to 4 minutes, stirring well after each minute. When the mixture is smooth, just spread it over the crackers and continue as above. And for a different serving idea, microwave the finished bars for 5 to 10 seconds right before serving and you'll have a warm, soft treat (but don't over-cook!).

*If you don't buy the pecans already toasted, it's easy to do it yourself: Spread out the pecans on a cookie sheet and bake at 350°F. just until lightly browned. (Keep an eye on them, 'cause it doesn't take too long!)

Desserts

Chocolate-Orange Pudding Parfaits

4 parfaits

From the navel orange growers, this one'll have your gang pleading for more . . . and more . . . and more! Oh, my!

1 package (4-serving size) chocolate instant pudding and pie filling

2 cups whole or lowfat milk

1 teaspoon fresh grated orange peel

1 navel orange, peeled and diced

4 teaspoons peanut butter (crunchy or smooth style)

Whipped topping (optional)

In a medium-sized bowl, whisk together the pudding mix and milk. Stir in the grated orange rind, then chill for 15 minutes. Assemble the parfaits by spooning 2 tablespoons of the chilled pudding mixture into each of 4 parfait glasses or dessert dishes. Evenly distribute half of the orange pieces over the pudding, then spoon 2 tablespoons more of the pudding mixture over the orange pieces. Spoon 1 teaspoon of peanut butter into the center of each parfait. Sprinkle on the remaining orange pieces, then spoon the remaining pudding over the orange pieces, covering them completely. Top with whipped topping, if desired. Serve immediately or cover and keep chilled until ready to serve.

Classic Deep-Dish Apple Pie

8 servings

*Apple pie is an American institution, and with just one taste of
this one you'll know why. Using a prepared deep-dish pie
crust takes away all of the hassle, so why not mix this
one up and easily enjoy all the applause?!*

2½ pounds Northern Spy, Cortland, or Granny Smith apples, peeled, cored, and sliced	1½ teaspoons ground cinnamon
	½ teaspoon ground nutmeg
	¼ cup all-purpose flour
1 cup sugar	1 deep-dish pie crust
	1 tablespoon butter, sliced into thirds

Preheat the oven to 425°F. Place the apple slices in a large bowl and add the sugar, cinnamon, nutmeg, and flour; mix well. Place the pie crust in a glass deep-dish pie plate, then pour the apple mixture into the crust. Dot with the butter and seal with the top crust. Cut slits in the top. Place the pie on a cookie sheet and bake for 15 minutes. Reduce the oven temperature to 350°F. and bake for 35 to 40 minutes more, or until the crust is golden.

Creamy Pumpkin Pie

8 servings

Think we couldn't get any better than our good ol' American pumpkin pie? Well, we did! And wait'll your dinner guests get hold of it!!

2	eggs, slightly beaten	1¼	teaspoons ground cinnamon	
1	can (16 ounces) solid-pack pumpkin	½	teaspoon ground nutmeg	
¾	cup sugar	¼	teaspoon ground cloves	
½	teaspoon salt	1	can (12 ounces) evaporated milk	
½	teaspoon ground ginger	1	unbaked 9-inch deep-dish pie shell	
1½	teaspoons all-purpose flour			

Preheat the oven to 425°F. In a large bowl, mix together all the ingredients, except the pie shell, then pour the mixture into the pie shell. Bake for 20 minutes, then reduce heat to 350°F. and bake for about 40 minutes more or until a knife inserted in the center comes out clean.

Crunchy Peanut Pie

8 servings

This proves that what they say is true: "Goodness grows in North Carolina." Why, peanuts never tasted so good!

3 eggs	½ teaspoon vanilla extract
½ cup sugar	1½ cups chopped dry roasted
½ cup dark corn syrup	peanuts
¼ cup (½ stick) butter, melted	1 unbaked 9-inch pie shell
¼ teaspoon salt	

Preheat the oven to 375°F. In a medium-sized bowl, beat the eggs until foamy. Add the sugar, corn syrup, butter, salt, and vanilla. Continue to beat until thoroughly blended. Stir in the peanuts. Place the pie shell on a cookie sheet, pour in the filling, and bake for 25 to 30 minutes, or until golden. Cool in the refrigerator and serve.

Crusty Blueberry Cobbler

6 servings

*Cobbler is classic New England, and this one
is classic delicious!!*

3 cups fresh blueberries	½ teaspoon ground cinnamon
2 teaspoons lemon juice	¼ teaspoon ground nutmeg
½ teaspoon vanilla extract	¼ cup (½ stick) butter for
1½ cups biscuit baking mix	dotting
¾ cup sugar	

Preheat the oven to 350°F. In a large bowl, toss together the blueberries, lemon juice, and vanilla. Spoon the mixture into a buttered 8-inch square baking pan. In a medium-sized bowl, combine the biscuit baking mix, sugar, cinnamon, and nutmeg. Sprinkle over the blueberry mixture, then dot with the butter. Bake for 45 to 55 minutes, or until just crispy.

NOTE: This is mouth-watering just as is or you can serve it with whipped cream, whipped topping, or ice cream.

Dirt Cups

8 to 10 servings

The kids will fight for these . . . that's how much fun they are!

2 cups cold milk

1 package (4-serving size) chocolate instant pudding and pie filling

1 container (8 ounces) frozen whipped topping, thawed

1 package (16 ounces) chocolate sandwich cookies, finely crushed

Gummy worms and frogs, candy flowers, chopped peanuts, and/or granola for decoration (optional)

Pour the milk into a large bowl. Add the pudding mix and, with a wire whisk, rotary beater, or electric mixer at lowest speed, beat for 1 to 2 minutes, or until well blended. Let stand for 5 minutes. Stir in the whipped topping and half of the crushed cookies. Place 1 tablespoon of the remaining crushed cookies into each of 8 to 10 seven-ounce paper or plastic cups. Fill each cup about ¾ full with the pudding mixture, then top with the remaining crushed cookies. Refrigerate for about 1 hour before serving. Decorate as desired.

NOTE: You can crush the cookies by hand or in a food processor. To make Sand Cups, substitute vanilla pudding for the chocolate pudding, a 12-ounce package of finely crushed vanilla cream-filled cookies or vanilla wafers for the chocolate sandwich cookies, and use gummy worms and sharks and/or chopped peanuts for decoration.

Frozen Lemon Loaf

8 to 10 servings

Easy, refreshing, and full of Florida sunshine.

15 vanilla wafers	½ cup lemon juice
1 can (14 ounces) sweetened condensed milk	1 container (8 ounces) frozen whipped topping, thawed

Line the bottom and sides of an 8" × 4" loaf pan with aluminum foil, extending the foil 1" over the edges of the pan. Arrange the vanilla wafers, top side down, on the bottom of the pan, overlapping to fit the bottom. In a large bowl, combine the sweetened condensed milk and the lemon juice. Fold in the whipped topping, then place the mixture over the vanilla wafers. Cover and freeze for 4 hours or until firm. Invert onto a serving plate and peel off the foil. If necessary, let stand for 10 minutes before slicing and serving. Store leftover loaf in the freezer.

Grapenut Pudding

about 8 servings

*Why wait till you take a trip to the Ocean State
(that's Rhode Island) or the other coastal areas
to enjoy this traditional New England favorite?*

1 cup grapenuts	½ cup sugar
2 cups milk, slightly warmed	¼ teaspoon salt
2 cups half-and-half	1 teaspoon vanilla extract
4 eggs, beaten	Ground nutmeg for garnish

Preheat the oven to 350°F. In a large bowl, combine all the ingredients, except the nutmeg. Pour the mixture into a greased 9-inch square baking pan, then sprinkle the top with nutmeg. Place the baking pan in a larger pan and add water to the larger pan, filling it halfway. Bake for 1 hour or until light golden and set. Let cool, then serve.

NOTE: Serve with dollops of whipped topping, if you'd like.

Grated Apple Pie

6 to 8 servings

Here's an apple pie that's different 'cause it uses grated apples,
so it gets nice and solid (that makes it easy to cut),
and it sure contains that same All-American fresh
OOH it's so GOOD™-ness!

1¼ cups sugar	½ cup (1 stick) butter, melted
3 tablespoons all-purpose flour	1 teaspoon vanilla extract
½ teaspoon ground cinnamon	3 cups coarsely grated apples (about 4 medium-sized apples)
½ teaspoon ground nutmeg	
2 eggs, beaten	1 unbaked 9-inch deep-dish pie shell

Preheat the oven to 400°F. In a large bowl, combine the sugar, flour, cinnamon, and nutmeg. Add the eggs, butter, and vanilla, then fold in the apples. Pour the mixture into the pie shell and bake for 10 minutes. Reduce the temperature to 350°F. and bake for 60 to 65 minutes more or until the top is golden. Cool completely and serve.

Harvest Cake

15 to 18 servings

Bringing in the harvest was never this scrumptious (till now)!!

1 package (12 ounces) frozen squash, thawed

3 cups all-purpose flour

2 cups sugar

2 teaspoons baking powder

2 teaspoons baking soda

2 teaspoons ground cinnamon

3 eggs

1 cup vegetable oil

1 cup (1 6-ounce package) semisweet chocolate chips

Preheat the oven to 350°F. In a large bowl, mix together all the ingredients. Pour into a greased 7" × 11" baking pan and bake for about 55 minutes, or until a wooden toothpick inserted in the center comes out clean.

Hawaiian Pudding Pie

6 to 8 servings

Until we can relax on a Hawaiian beach, this gives us some of that warm sunshiny feeling.

1 large package (6-serving size) vanilla instant pudding and pie filling*

2 cups milk

2 tablespoons melted butter

1 cup frozen whipped topping, thawed (1 8-ounce container equals 3½ cups)

1 prepared 9-inch graham cracker pie crust

½ cup toasted flaked coconut (optional)

In a large bowl, prepare the pudding according to the package directions, using the 2 cups milk. Fold in the butter and whipped topping, then pour the mixture into the pie crust. Refrigerate for 4 hours, or until firm. Top with the toasted coconut just before serving, if desired.

NOTE: Every time you make this it can be a different kind of pie . . . for instance, why not line the bottom of the pie crust with banana slices, berries, peaches, or canned fruit before adding the filling? And if you'd like to make your own toasted coconut, spread out the flaked coconut on a cookie sheet and bake at 325°F. until golden brown, mixing occasionally.

*If you have only the 4-serving-size packages on hand, then open 2 of them and measure out and use ⅔ cup pudding mix.

Johnny Appleseed Cake

18 to 24 servings

*All of us apple lovers owe Johnny Appleseed a big thanks
for his delicious deeds.*

1 box (18.25 ounces) yellow
  cake mix

1 can (21 ounces) apple pie
  filling

4 eggs

Preheat the oven to 350°F. In a large bowl, mix together all the ingredients by hand or with an electric mixer. Pour evenly into a greased 9" × 13" baking dish and bake for 35 to 40 minutes or until a wooden toothpick inserted in the center comes out clean.

NOTE: Any combination of cake mix and pie filling will work. Use your imagination to come up with your own favorite taste treats.

Layered Brownies

about 24 brownies

These are for certified brownie lovers—no impostors, please!!

BROWNIE LAYER

4   1-ounce squares *unsweetened* chocolate

¾   cup (1½ sticks) butter

2   cups granulated sugar

3   eggs, beaten

1   teaspoon vanilla extract

1   cup all-purpose flour

1   cup chopped peanuts

PEANUT BUTTER LAYER

1   cup peanut butter

½   cup confectioners' sugar

1   teaspoon vanilla extract

GLAZE

4   1-ounce squares *semisweet* chocolate

¼   cup (½ stick) butter

Preheat the oven to 350°F. In a large microwaveable bowl, heat the unsweetened chocolate and the ¾ cup butter in the microwave on high for 2 minutes (or melt in a saucepan on the stove over low heat), just until the butter is melted. Stir until the chocolate is completely melted. Stir in the granulated sugar, then mix in the beaten eggs and 1 teaspoon vanilla until well blended. Stir in the flour and peanuts, then spread into a greased 9" × 13" baking pan. Bake for 30 to 35 minutes or until a wooden toothpick inserted in the center comes out with fudgy crumbs. **Do not overbake.** Cool in the pan.

Meanwhile, in a medium-sized bowl, combine the Peanut Butter Layer ingredients until well blended and smooth. Spread over the cooled brownies.

Place the Glaze ingredients in a small microwaveable bowl and heat in the microwave on high for 2 minutes (or melt in a saucepan on the stove over low heat), just until the butter is melted. Stir until the chocolate is completely melted. Spread over the Peanut Butter Layer. Cool until set, then cut into squares.

Lemon Cheese Bars

24 bars

*If this doesn't make you feel the Arizona sunshine,
nothing will!*

1 box (18.25 ounces) yellow cake mix with pudding

2 eggs

⅓ cup vegetable oil

1 package (8 ounces) cream cheese, softened

⅓ cup sugar

1 teaspoon fresh lemon juice

Preheat the oven to 350°F. In a medium-sized bowl, combine the cake mix, 1 egg, and the oil; mix until crumbly. Reserve 1 cup of the mixture. Lightly pat the remaining mixture into an ungreased 9" × 13" baking pan. Bake for 15 minutes; cool slightly. Meanwhile, in another medium-sized bowl, beat together the remaining egg, cream cheese, sugar, and lemon juice until light and smooth. Spread over the cooled baked layer. Sprinkle with the reserved crumb mixture and bake for 15 minutes more, or until light golden. Cool, then cut into bars.

Lime Margarita Bars

28 bars

*A cool Southwestern dessert to top off a spicy Southwestern
(or any) meal. It sure is a dessert with a difference!*

2 cups finely crushed pretzels (about 8 ounces)	2 cans (14 ounces each) sweetened condensed milk
¼ cup sugar	3 eggs, lightly beaten
½ cup (1 stick) butter, melted	½ cup fresh lime juice
	4 teaspoons grated lime peel

Preheat the oven to 350°F. Line a 9" × 13" baking pan with foil, allowing the foil to hang over the short sides. Butter the foil and set aside. In a medium-sized bowl, combine the pretzels, sugar, and butter. Firmly press over the bottom of the prepared pan. Bake until the crust is firm, about 10 minutes; cool slightly. Meanwhile, in a large bowl, combine the remaining ingredients. Pour into the cooled crust. Bake for 25 to 30 minutes or until the center is firm. Cool completely on a wire rack. Pull up the ends of the foil to remove from pan. Cut into bars.

NOTE: These freeze well, but be sure to place them in a tightly covered container. When ready to serve, just remove as many as needed and thaw at room temperature for 30 minutes.

Lowfat Carrot Cake

12 to 15 servings

These days, everybody wants recipes with less fat.
Well, this one does it . . . deliciously!

4 cups shredded carrots (not firmly packed)

2 cups sugar

1 can (8 ounces) crushed pineapple, drained

1 cup prune purée or prepared prune butter

4 egg whites

2 teaspoons vanilla extract

2 cups all-purpose flour

2 teaspoons baking soda

2 teaspoons ground cinnamon

½ teaspoon salt

¾ cup shredded or flaked coconut

Preheat the oven to 375°F. In a large bowl, combine the carrots, sugar, pineapple, prune purée, egg whites, and vanilla. Stir to blend thoroughly. Add the remaining ingredients except the coconut. Mix completely. Gently stir in the coconut. Spread the batter into a 9" × 13" baking pan that has been coated with nonstick vegetable spray. Bake for about 40 minutes or until a wooden toothpick inserted in the center comes out clean. Cool on a rack, then cut into squares.

NOTE: Using prune purée or prepared prune butter in place of oil allows us to enjoy baked goods that are low in fat, yet are rich, moist, and flavorful. Use it in a direct one-to-one substitution for butter, margarine, or oil in darker baked goods. Prune purée and prune butter are available ready to use (found in the jam & jelly or baking section of your supermarket), or you can make your own purée by combining 1⅓ cups (8 ounces) pitted prunes and 6 tablespoons water in the container of a food processor; pulse on and off until the mixture is smooth. It makes 1 cup.

Lowfat Fudgy Brownies

12 to 16 brownies

You might as well keep it secret that these scrumptious treats are low in fat—'cause no one will believe you!!

4 ounces unsweetened chocolate

½ cup prune purée or prepared prune butter

3 egg whites

1 cup sugar

1 teaspoon salt

1 teaspoon vanilla extract

½ cup all-purpose flour

¼ cup chopped walnuts

Preheat the oven to 350°F. Cut the chocolate into 1-inch pieces and melt in the microwave or on the stove in a saucepan over low heat, stirring occasionally, just until the chocolate is melted. (Do not allow to boil.) Remove from heat and place in a large bowl; add the remaining ingredients, except the flour and nuts. Beat to blend thoroughly. Mix in the flour. Spread the batter in an 8-inch square baking pan that has been coated with nonstick vegetable spray; sprinkle with the walnuts. Bake for about 30 minutes or until springy to the touch. Cool on a rack and cut into squares.

NOTE: See previous page about using prune purée or prepared prune butter in place of oil.

Lower-Fat Whipped Topping

3 to 4 cups

Yes, a lot of us are weight-conscious, but who says we can't enjoy a treat once in a while, especially something that's lower in fat? This is the new trick for getting a lowfat substitute for whipped cream. Give it a try and see what you think.

1   cup evaporated skimmed milk   1   teaspoon vanilla extract
½ cup confectioners' sugar

Pour the evaporated milk into a small glass bowl. Along with beaters, chill the evaporated milk in the freezer for about an hour, or until ice crystals form around the edge of the bowl. (It's okay if it freezes slightly.) Beat on high for about 1 minute or until very frothy. Gradually add the confectioners' sugar and vanilla; continue beating for 2 to 3 minutes or until firm. Use immediately.

NOTE: This is a great way to enjoy whipped topping that's lower in fat and calories than the regular . . . but be sure to make it right before serving so that it holds together.

Microwave Maple "Baked" Apples

5 servings

This combination of apples and maple syrup makes me think of autumn in Vermont.

5 red baking apples, cored   5 tablespoons maple syrup
1 cup apple cider or juice   Ground cinnamon for topping

Remove a small spiral peel from the top of each apple with a paring knife. Place the apples in a microwaveable casserole dish, leaving space between them. Pour the apple cider over and around the apples. Drizzle about 1 tablespoon of syrup over each apple, then dust lightly with cinnamon. Cover tightly and microwave on high for 5 minutes, then turn the casserole dish and microwave on high for 5 minutes more, or until fork tender.

NOTE: Serve with a dollop of vanilla yogurt, ice cream, or whipped topping, if desired. Decorate topped apples for holiday fun!

Mississippi Mud Pie

8 to 10 servings

The banks of the Mississippi are muddy, all right . . . and this
pie is just as thick and rich as its namesake.

1 quart of your favorite ice cream, softened to spreading consistency (coffee is the traditional flavor)

1 prepared 9-inch chocolate-flavored pie crust

1 container (8 ounces) frozen whipped topping, thawed

Chocolate syrup for drizzling

Chopped nuts for sprinkling (optional)

Spoon the softened ice cream into the pie crust. Freeze until firm, about 2 hours. Top with the whipped topping, drizzle with chocolate syrup and chopped nuts, if desired. Freeze until solid, about 1 hour. Slice and serve or keep frozen until ready to use. Allow to thaw for 5 to 10 minutes for easier slicing.

NOTE: To soften the ice cream, break it up in a bowl and stir with a wooden spoon. Do not let the ice cream reach the melting point.

New Orleans Bread Pudding with Bourbon Sauce

8 to 10 servings

You'll feel like you're in the middle of Bourbon Street when you hear the cheers for this. Do it . . . make dessert a Mardi Gras!!

1 quart whole milk
1 loaf French bread, broken into pieces
3 eggs
2 cups sugar
2 tablespoons vanilla extract
1 cup raisins

BOURBON SAUCE

½ cup (1 stick) butter
1 can (5 ounces) evaporated milk (⅔ cup)
1 cup sugar
1 egg yolk, beaten
2 tablespoons bourbon

Preheat the oven to 400°F. Pour the milk into a large bowl; add the bread, crushing with the back of a spoon, and soak until all the milk is absorbed. Add the 3 whole eggs, 2 cups sugar, vanilla, and raisins; mix well. Spread the mixture evenly into an 8-inch square baking dish that has been coated with nonstick vegetable spray. Bake for 40 to 50 minutes, or until firm and golden. Before serving, combine the Bourbon Sauce ingredients, except the bourbon, in a medium-sized saucepan. Cook over low heat, stirring constantly, for 10 to 15 minutes, or until thickened. Stir in the bourbon. Serve warm over the bread pudding.

New York Easy Cheesecake

12 to 16 servings

*There's no cheesecake like New York cheesecake. And there's no
New York–style cheesecake recipe as easy as this.
(Two more great reasons to love New York!)*

3 packages (8 ounces each)
   cream cheese, softened
1 cup sugar
4 eggs
1 teaspoon vanilla extract
2 prepared 9-inch graham
   cracker pie crusts

TOPPING

3 tablespoons sugar
1 pint (16 ounces) sour cream
1 teaspoon vanilla extract
¼ teaspoon lemon juice

Preheat the oven to 375°F. In a large bowl, blend the cream
cheese and 1 cup sugar with an electric mixer. Add the eggs, one at
a time, then 1 teaspoon of vanilla; mix well. Pour evenly into the
pie crusts and bake for 40 to 45 minutes, or until firm. Remove from
the oven and allow to cool for 5 minutes. Meanwhile, in a medium-
sized bowl, beat the topping ingredients until well blended. Pour
evenly over the pies and bake for an additional 5 minutes. Cool,
then refrigerate for 24 hours before serving.

Orange Bars

about 18 bars

A bit of a Texas kid's fun in every delicious bite!

2¼ cups firmly packed brown
   sugar
2   cups all-purpose flour, plus
   2 tablespoons for coating
¼   teaspoon salt
4   eggs, beaten

½ cup vegetable oil
½ pound orange jelly candy
   slices
1 cup finely chopped walnuts
½ cup confectioners' sugar

Preheat the oven to 350°F. In a medium-sized bowl, combine the brown sugar, 2 cups flour, and salt. Add the eggs and oil; mix well and set aside. Coat the candy slices with the remaining 2 tablespoons flour, then cut the candy into small pieces and add to the batter, along with the nuts; mix just until combined. Pour the batter into a well-greased and floured 7" × 11" baking dish. Bake for about 50 minutes, or until golden and a wooden toothpick inserted in the center comes out clean. Remove from the oven and let cool slightly. Before completely cooled, cut into squares. Place the confectioners' sugar in a plastic bag; put a few squares at a time into the plastic bag and shake to coat the bars. Serve immediately or store in an airtight container until ready to serve (because they dry out quickly).

Poppy Seed Cake

12 to 16 servings

So moist and light, you'd better make two.
One for them, and one for you!

1 box (18.5 ounces) butter cake mix or 1 box (18.25 ounces) yellow cake mix

1 box (4-serving size) instant vanilla pudding and pie filling

1 cup water

½ cup vegetable oil

4 eggs

3 tablespoons poppy seed

1 teaspoon almond extract

1 teaspoon butter flavor

ICING

2 cups confectioners' sugar (about ½ of a 16-ounce box)

1 tablespoon butter, melted

2 tablespoons heavy cream

1 teaspoon vanilla extract

2 tablespoons milk

Preheat the oven to 350°F. In a large bowl, mix together the cake mix and pudding mix. Add the water and oil; beat well. Add the eggs, one at a time, beating after each addition. Add the poppy seed, almond, and butter flavors. Bake in a greased 12-cup Bundt pan for 45 to 50 minutes or until a wooden toothpick inserted in the center comes out clean. Cool on a rack for 30 minutes before removing from the pan. Meanwhile, in a medium-sized bowl, combine all the icing ingredients. Once the cake is cool, drizzle with the icing.

Quakertown Crumb Pie

6 to 8 servings

You're sure to gain lots of friends with this popular
Pennsylvania pie. It's old-fashioned
goodness from simpler times.

¼ cup plus ⅓ cup firmly
    packed brown sugar, divided
¼ cup molasses
1 egg, lightly beaten
1½ cups water
1 cup plus 2 tablespoons all-
    purpose flour, divided

1¼ teaspoons vanilla extract
½ teaspoon baking soda
¼ cup (½ stick) butter, melted
⅛ teaspoon ground cinnamon
1 unbaked 9-inch pie shell

Preheat the oven to 375°F. In a small saucepan, combine ¼ cup brown sugar, the molasses, egg, water, and the 2 tablespoons flour. Cook over medium heat, stirring constantly, until the mixture thickens. Remove from the heat, cool for 5 minutes, then stir in the vanilla; set aside. In a large bowl, combine the remaining 1 cup flour with the baking soda; add the remaining ⅓ cup brown sugar, the melted butter, and cinnamon, stirring with a fork until crumbly. Pour the molasses mixture into the pie shell; top with the crumb mixture, sprinkling evenly. Bake for 40 to 45 minutes, or until light golden. Cool before serving.

Raisin Pumpkin Cake

about 12 servings

Feel the crispness of autumn anytime of the year.

2 cups all-purpose flour
2 cups granulated sugar
2 teaspoons baking powder
1 teaspoon baking soda
2 teaspoons pumpkin pie spice
½ teaspoon salt
4 eggs, beaten

1 can (16 ounces) solid-pack pumpkin (2 cups)
¾ cup vegetable oil
2 cups All-Bran® cereal
1 cup raisins
1 cup chopped walnuts or pecans
Confectioners' sugar for topping (optional)

Preheat the oven to 350°F. In a large bowl, combine the flour, sugar, baking powder, baking soda, pumpkin pie spice, and salt. In another large bowl, mix together the beaten eggs, pumpkin, vegetable oil, and cereal. Add the flour mixture to the pumpkin mixture, mixing just until combined. Stir in the raisins and nuts. Pour the mixture evenly into a 10" × 4" tube pan or a 12-cup Bundt pan that has been coated with nonstick vegetable spray. Bake for about 65 minutes or until a wooden toothpick inserted in the center comes out clean. Cool completely and remove from the pan. Dust with confectioners' sugar, if desired.

Roaring Twenties Cake

9 servings

Careful!! Your family may have an irresistible urge
to dance the Charleston!!

2 cups firmly packed brown sugar

2 cups hot water

¼ cup (½ stick) butter

½ of a 15-ounce box of raisins (about 1¼ cups)

1 teaspoon salt

2 teaspoons ground cinnamon

2 teaspoons ground cloves

1 tablespoon lukewarm water

2 teaspoons baking soda

3 cups all-purpose flour

Preheat the oven to 350°F. In a medium-sized saucepan, combine the sugar, hot water, butter, raisins, salt, cinnamon, and cloves; bring to a boil and cook for 5 minutes, stirring occasionally. Remove from the heat and set aside to cool. When cool, add the lukewarm water, baking soda, and flour; mix well. Pour into an 8-inch square baking pan that has been coated with nonstick vegetable spray and bake for 30 to 35 minutes, or until a wooden toothpick inserted in the center comes out clean.

Rocky Road Pie

6 to 8 servings

Chocoholic alert!! This one's for you—and me. Please share!

2 packages (4-serving size each) instant chocolate pudding and pie filling mix

½ cup semisweet chocolate chips

2 cups miniature marshmallows

1 prepared 9-inch chocolate-flavored pie crust

1 container (8 ounces) frozen whipped topping, thawed

Chopped walnuts or other nuts for garnish

Prepare the chocolate pudding according to the package directions and place in a large bowl. Mix in the chocolate chips and marshmallows. Pour into the pie crust and top with whipped topping and nuts. Serve, or cover and refrigerate until ready to serve.

Shoofly Pie

12 to 16 servings

*This was born in the heart of the Pennsylvania Dutch countryside,
but word quickly spread to other areas—you'll see why!*

1 cup water	CRUMB MIX
1 rounded teaspoon instant coffee	3 cups all-purpose flour
1 teaspoon baking soda	¾ cup firmly packed brown sugar
1 cup dark corn syrup	⅓ cup butter-flavored vegetable shortening
2 tablespoons molasses, divided (optional)	
2 unbaked 9-inch pie shells	

Preheat the oven to 350°F. Boil the water in a medium-sized saucepan. Dissolve the coffee in the boiling water. Turn off the heat, then mix in the baking soda and corn syrup. If using molasses, evenly spread 1 tablespoon over the bottom of each pie shell, then pour the coffee mixture evenly into both shells. In a large bowl, combine the flour and brown sugar. Using a fork, cut in the vegetable shortening until the mixture is crumbly. Sprinkle the Crumb Mix evenly over the pies, place the pies on a cookie sheet, and bake for 55 minutes or until the crusts are light brown.

Sparkling Lemon Ice

4 to 6 servings

Whew!! A refreshing, easy way to bring down the summer heat.

1 package (4-serving size) lemon-flavored gelatin
1 cup boiling water
1 cup cold lemon-lime seltzer

3 tablespoons fresh lemon juice
½ teaspoon grated lemon peel

Dissolve the gelatin completely in the boiling water. Add the seltzer, lemon juice, and lemon peel. Pour into a 9-inch square pan, cover, and freeze for 3 hours or until frozen. Remove from the freezer and let stand at room temperature for 10 minutes. Beat on medium speed with an electric mixer or process in a food processor until smooth. Spoon into dessert dishes and serve.

NOTE: Try any other fruit-flavored gelatin—or try making a few flavors at the same time for a refreshing dessert smorgasbord.

"That Cherry Stuff"

8 to 10 servings

I cannot tell a lie—I love this! And you will, too. . .
not only for the taste, but for all the fun
you'll have making and eating it.

1 can (21 ounces) cherry pie
filling

1 container (8 ounces) frozen
whipped topping, thawed

1 can (14 ounces) sweetened
condensed milk

1 can (8 ounces) crushed
pineapple, drained

1 cup coarsely chopped nuts
(any kind)

In a large bowl, fold together all the ingredients. Spoon into a
serving bowl or individual dessert glasses. Chill before serving.

Vanilla Cream Pie

6 to 8 servings

Smooth, cool, and luscious—what more could you want?
Okay, it's quick and easy, too!

1 can (14 ounces) sweetened condensed milk	½ cup sour cream
¼ cup water	1 container (8 ounces) frozen whipped topping, thawed
1 box (4-serving size) vanilla instant pudding and pie filling	1 prepared 9-inch graham cracker pie crust

In a large bowl, combine the sweetened condensed milk, water, and pudding mix; mix for about 30 seconds or until the pudding is dissolved. Do not overmix. Fold in the sour cream, then fold in the whipped topping. Pour the mixture into the pie crust and refrigerate for at least 8 hours, or overnight.

NOTE: Why not try placing about 1 cup blueberries or peach slices directly on the crust before adding the filling? It makes for an extra-fresh summer treat!

All-American Kitchen Sink

8 to 10 appetizer-sized servings

This really does call for almost "everything but the kitchen sink"—and wait till everybody starts squealing and cheering . . . you'll see.

1 loaf Italian bread	½ of a small onion, chopped
½ cup prepared mustard	1½ cups sliced mushrooms
½ cup brown sugar, lightly packed	1 can (8 ounces) crushed pineapple, in its own juice, drained well until all liquid is removed
8 ounces thinly sliced ham or smoked turkey	
2 medium-sized tomatoes, cored and thinly sliced	2 cups (8 ounces) shredded mozzarella cheese
½ of a green or red bell pepper, chopped	

Preheat the oven to 400°F. Cut the bread in half lengthwise. Remove excess bread from the center of each half, leaving a boat shape with a ½-inch-thick shell. Place on a 10" × 15" cookie sheet and toast until golden, about 10 minutes. Meanwhile, in a small bowl, combine the mustard and brown sugar, stirring until the sugar is dissolved. Spread the mustard mixture evenly over the toasted bread shells. Top with the ham, tomatoes, bell pepper, onion, mushrooms, drained pineapple, and mozzarella cheese. Bake for about 20 minutes, or until heated through and the cheese is bubbly.

Blackened Seasoning Blend

about ¼ cup

When we hear that something's got a blackened Cajun flavoring,
we get ready for spicy, crispy, and yummy.
This is the one that'll do it.

1 tablespoon paprika	1 teaspoon salt
2 teaspoons dried thyme leaves, crushed	1 teaspoon sugar
	½ teaspoon cayenne pepper
1 teaspoon onion powder	1 teaspoon black pepper
1 teaspoon garlic powder	

In a small bowl, combine all the ingredients and mix well. Store in a tightly covered jar.

NOTE: For great Cajun taste without all the smoke, sprinkle this on fish, meats, or chicken toward the end of broiling or sautéing. This recipe can easily be doubled or tripled; make it hotter or milder to your taste by varying the amounts of the individual ingredients.

Campfire Pancakes

about 15 medium-sized pancakes

The tastes and smells of a crackling campfire can't really be
duplicated, but when you make these at home on your own
griddle you can get pretty close. See ya' this summer,
Deloris . . . have some ready for me, please!

3 eggs, well beaten
2 cups milk
3 tablespoons vegetable oil
3 cups all-purpose flour

3 teaspoons baking powder
½ teaspoon salt
2 tablespoons sugar

In a medium-sized bowl, combine the eggs, milk, and oil. In a
large bowl, combine the remaining ingredients; add the egg mixture
and mix thoroughly with a wooden spoon until smooth. Pour ⅓ cup
of the batter onto a well-greased, hot skillet or griddle for each pancake. When bubbles form and the edges begin to brown, flip the
pancakes and brown the other side.

Cheese Stack

about 8 servings

*Southwestern flavors for true cheese lovers. It's so easy,
but the finished wedges make you look like
a professional chef.*

1½ cups cottage cheese
(1 16-ounce container yields
about 2 cups)

1 pint (16 ounces) sour cream,
divided

3 cups (12 ounces) shredded
mozzarella cheese, divided

¾ cup grated Parmesan cheese

1 can (4 ounces) chopped green
chilies

4 flour tortillas (8 to 10 inches)

1 tablespoon sliced ripe olives

2 scallions, sliced

8 to 10 cherry tomatoes, cut in
half

Preheat the oven to 350°F. In a large bowl, combine the cottage cheese, 1½ cups sour cream, 2 cups mozzarella cheese, the Parmesan cheese, and green chilies. Grease the bottom and sides of a deep-dish pie plate (or a round baking dish that's about the same size as the tortillas). Place one tortilla in the pie plate and cover with ⅓ of the cheese mixture (about 1⅓ cups). Repeat the layers, ending with a tortilla. Bake for 20 minutes, or until the cheeses melt and just begin to bubble out from between the tortillas. Remove from the oven and sprinkle with the reserved cup of mozzarella cheese. Return to the oven and bake for 5 minutes more. Remove from the oven and garnish the top with the olives, scallions, and tomatoes. Cut into wedges and serve topped with the remaining sour cream.

Corn Pancakes

about 8 pancakes

When I think about the Midwest, one of the things that comes to mind is the vision of cornfields that seem to go on forever. Here's a recipe that'll give you some of that traditional corn goodness, easily!

2 cups cooked corn kernels
(about 3 to 4 ears)

2 eggs, beaten

2 tablespoons butter, melted

2 tablespoons milk

½ teaspoon salt

½ cup all-purpose flour

In a large bowl, combine the corn, eggs, butter, milk, and salt; mix well. Stir in the flour, blending well. For each pancake, place ¼ cup batter onto a hot, lightly greased griddle or skillet. When the edges begin to brown, flip the pancakes and brown the other side.

NOTE: One 10-ounce package of frozen corn, thawed, will work just as well here. Serve with syrup, jam, or your favorite pancake topping.

Creole Seasoning

about ⅓ cup

*This can be the secret ingredient that gives any of
your dishes that perfect Louisiana touch.*

2	tablespoons cayenne pepper	1½	teaspoons ground coriander
4½	teaspoons salt	1½	teaspoons black pepper
1½	teaspoons chili powder	1	teaspoon ground cloves
1½	teaspoons paprika	¾	teaspoon garlic powder

In a small bowl, blend together all the ingredients. Place in a tightly covered container and store in a cool place.

NOTE: Serving options include:

★ Sprinkle ¼ teaspoon on each side of a 1-pound steak before cooking.
★ Sprinkle ¼ teaspoon (no more!) on 4 servings of buttered cooked vegetables.
★ Add ¼ teaspoon to ¼ cup mayonnaise for a zippy dressing.

Fruit-Filled Trail Mix

about 8 cups

A yummy twist on the original cereal snack mix. . .
for kids of all ages!

3	cups popped popcorn	1	tablespoon soy sauce
2	cups pretzel sticks	½	teaspoon ground ginger (optional)
2	cups bite-sized corn cereal squares	1¼	cups (5 to 6 ounces) assorted bite-sized fruit snacks
¼	cup (½ stick) butter, melted		

Preheat the oven to 275°F. In a large bowl, combine the popcorn, pretzel sticks, and cereal squares. In a small bowl, blend the butter, soy sauce, and ginger; drizzle over the cereal mixture, stirring until coated. Spread evenly onto a 10" × 15" rimmed cookie sheet. Bake for 30 minutes, stirring carefully every 10 minutes. Cool slightly, then combine with the fruit snacks.

NOTE: Great for parties or between-meal snacks.

Hawaiian Fruit Dip

about 1½ cups

Aloha! Dip into a tropical paradise treat.
Mmm, so cool and delicious!

1 can (8 ounces) crushed
pineapple in its own juice,
undrained

1 package (4-serving size)
instant coconut-cream
pudding mix

¾ cup milk

½ cup sour cream

In a blender or food processor, combine all the ingredients; blend for 30 seconds. Transfer the mixture to a small bowl, cover, and refrigerate for several hours or overnight, allowing the flavors to blend.

NOTE: Great for dipping fresh fruit such as melon, strawberries, peaches, and nectarines.

Tropical Cranberry Juice

8 cups

*Just one sip and you'll swear you're on vacation in the
tropics . . . with a touch of Cape Cod thrown in.*

4 cups orange juice
4 cups cranberry juice cocktail

1 teaspoon banana extract

Combine all the ingredients in a large pitcher. Chill and serve.

White Pizza

3 to 4 servings

It's the rage in restaurants and pizza shops across the country, but why not make it at home tonight? (Yes, it's that easy!)

1	large Italian bread shell (like Boboli®)	2	cups (8 ounces) shredded mozzarella cheese
2	cups mushroom slices	½	teaspoon Italian seasoning
¼	cup (½ stick) butter, melted	¼	teaspoon garlic powder
1	tablespoon grated Parmesan cheese	¼	teaspoon onion powder

Preheat the oven to 375°F. Place the bread shell on an ungreased 12-inch pizza pan. In a medium-sized bowl, toss the mushrooms with the butter. Arrange the mushrooms over the shell, then sprinkle with the Parmesan and mozzarella cheeses, Italian seasoning, garlic and onion powders. Bake for 15 to 20 minutes, or until the cheese is melted and light golden.

Yogurt Cheese

¾ cup

*If you think you couldn't get excited by a cheese spread made of yogurt,
be prepared to change your mind. You won't believe
how good it tastes (and it's good for you, too)!*

> 1 container (16 ounces) plain
> lowfat or nonfat yogurt (with
> no added gelatin or thickeners)

Line a large wire strainer with a large paper coffee filter or 2 to 3 sheets of white paper towel; place the strainer over a deep bowl. Add the yogurt, then cover with plastic wrap. Refrigerate until the liquid has drained into the bowl and the yogurt has thickened to a spreadable consistency, about 8 hours. (There should be about 8 ounces of liquid; discard the drained liquid.) Transfer the yogurt cheese to a small bowl and store, covered, in the refrigerator until ready to serve.

NOTE: You can use this as you would any cheese spread, or try it with the next two recipes.

Yogurt Cheese and Apricot Spread

about 1 cup

¾ cup yogurt cheese (see above)   ⅓ cup apricot preserves

In a medium-sized bowl, combine the yogurt cheese and the apricot preserves. Store, covered, in the refrigerator until ready to use.

NOTE: Use on toast, pancakes, fruit, or whatever strikes your fancy.

Yogurt and Blue Cheese Dip with Fruit

about 1½ cups

¾ cup yogurt cheese (page 287)
1 to 2 tablespoons crumbled
   blue cheese

¾ cup peeled, cored, and grated
   sweet apple or pear
½ teaspoon sugar
⅛ teaspoon salt

In a medium-sized bowl, mix together all the ingredients. Cover and store in the refrigerator until ready to use.

NOTE: Serve with sliced fresh vegetables or with apple and pear slices.

The following 2 recipes are made by mixing all of the ingredients together, then draining the *entire* mixture for about 8 hours.

Cinnamon-Raisin Yogurt Spread

about 1 cup

1 16-ounce or 2 8-ounce
   containers vanilla lowfat or
   nonfat yogurt (with no added
   gelatin or thickeners)

2 tablespoons golden raisins
2 teaspoons sugar
1 teaspoon ground cinnamon

Line a large wire strainer with a large paper coffee filter or 2 to 3 sheets of white paper towel. Place the strainer over a deep bowl; set aside. In another bowl, combine all the ingredients; spoon into the prepared strainer. Cover with plastic wrap and refrigerate until the liquid has drained into the bowl and the yogurt mixture has thickened to a spreadable consistency, about 8 hours. Discard the drained liquid. Transfer the yogurt spread to a small bowl and store, covered, in the refrigerator until ready to serve.

NOTE: Serve on bagels, toast, or English muffins.

Chive Yogurt Spread

about 1 cup

1 16-ounce or 2 8-ounce containers plain lowfat or nonfat yogurt (with no added gelatin or thickeners)

2 tablespoons mayonnaise

4 teaspoons chopped fresh chives or scallions

¼ teaspoon sugar

Prepare and serve as you would the Cinnamon-Raisin Yogurt Spread.

Index

Index

Mr. Food®

Can Help You Be A Kitchen Hero!

**Let Mr. Food® make your life easier with
Quick, No-Fuss Recipes and Helpful Kitchen Tips for**

Family Dinners • Soups and Salads • Potluck Dishes
Barbecues • Special Brunches • Unbelievable Desserts

. . . and that's just the beginning!

Complete your **Mr. Food®** cookbook library today.
It's so simple to share in all the
"OOH IT'S SO GOOD!!™"

✂ -

TITLE	PRICE	QUANTITY	
A. **Mr. Food®** Cooks Like Mama	@ $12.95 each	x _____	= $_____
B. The **Mr. Food®** Cookbook, *OOH IT'S SO GOOD!!™*	@ $12.95 each	x _____	= $_____
C. **Mr. Food®** Cooks Chicken	@ $ 9.95 each	x _____	= $_____
D. **Mr. Food®** Cooks Pasta	@ $ 9.95 each	x _____	= $_____
E. **Mr. Food®** Makes Dessert	@ $ 9.95 each	x _____	= $_____
F. **Mr. Food®** Cooks Real American	@ $14.95 each	x _____	= $_____
G. **Mr. Food®'s** Favorite Cookies	@ $11.95 each	x _____	= $_____
H. **Mr. Food®'s** Quick and Easy Side Dishes	@ $11.95 each	x _____	= $_____
I. **Mr. Food®** Grills It All in a Snap	@ $11.95 each	x _____	= $_____
J. **Mr. Food®'s** Fun Kitchen Tips and Shortcuts (and Recipes, Too!)	@ $11.95 each	x _____	= $_____
K. **Mr. Food®'s** Old World Cooking Made Easy	@ $14.95 each	x _____	= $_____
L. "Help, **Mr. Food®**! Company's Coming!"	@ $14.95 each	x _____	= $_____
M. **Mr. Food®** Pizza 1-2-3	@ $11.95 each	x _____	= $_____
N. **Mr. Food®** Meat Around the Table	@ $11.95 each	x _____	= $_____
O. **Mr. Food®** Simply Chocolate	@ $11.95 each	x _____	= $_____

Call 1-800-619-FOOD (3663) or send payment to:
Mr. Food®
P.O. Box 696
Holmes, PA 19043

Name _____

Street _____ Apt._____

City _____ State_____ Zip_____

Method of Payment: ☐ Check or Money Order Enclosed

☐ Credit Card: ☐ Visa ☐ MasterCard Expiration Date _____

Signature _____

Account #: ☐☐☐☐☐☐☐☐☐☐☐☐☐☐☐☐

Book Total	$_____
+$2.95 Postage & Handling First Copy **AND** $1 Ea. Add'l. Copy (Canadian Orders Add Add'l. $2.00 *Per Copy*)	$_____
Subtotal	$_____
Less $1.00 per book if ordering 3 or more books with this order	$ –_____
Add Applicable Sales Tax (FL Residents Only)	$_____
Total in U.S. Funds	$_____

Please allow 4 to 6 weeks for delivery.

BKF1